Alfred J. Wyatt

**An Elementary Old English Grammar**

Early West Saxon

Alfred J. Wyatt

**An Elementary Old English Grammar**
*Early West Saxon*

ISBN/EAN: 9783337081386

Printed in Europe, USA, Canada, Australia, Japan

Cover: Foto ©Paul-Georg Meister /pixelio.de

More available books at **www.hansebooks.com**

*BY THE SAME AUTHOR.*

**The Old English Lay of Beowulf.** Edited with Critical and Philological Notes and Alphabetical Glossary by A. J. WYATT, M.A., late Scholar of Christ's College, Cambridge; M.A. Lond. Crown 8vo. 8s. 6d.

**An Elementary Old English Reader.** [*In preparation.*

**An Old English Anthology.** [*In preparation.*

# AN ELEMENTARY
# OLD ENGLISH GRAMMAR

(EARLY WEST SAXON).

London: C. J. CLAY AND SONS,
CAMBRIDGE UNIVERSITY PRESS WAREHOUSE,
AVE MARIA LANE.
Glasgow: 263, ARGYLE STREET.

Leipzig: F. A. BROCKHAUS.
New York: THE MACMILLAN CO.
Bombay: GEORGE BELL AND SONS.

# OLD ENGLISH GRAMMAR

(EARLY WEST SAXON)

BY

A. J. WYATT,

M.A. (CANTAB. ET LOND.),

LATE SCHOLAR OF CHRIST'S COLLEGE, CAMBRIDGE,
EXTERNAL EXAMINER IN ENGLISH TO VICTORIA UNIVERSITY.

CAMBRIDGE:
AT THE UNIVERSITY PRESS.
1897

[*All Rights reserved.*]

Cambridge:
PRINTED BY J. AND C. F. CLAY,
AT THE UNIVERSITY PRESS.

# PREFACE.

OLD English Grammar has hitherto been taught in three ways, which may be called respectively the Germanic, the Gothic, and the independent methods. Sievers assumes that the student possesses a certain knowledge of Germanic, and makes it the basis of his classifications; Cosijn believes that the ready way to the Old English tongue is to learn Gothic first—a theory not difficult to reduce *ad absurdum*. Sweet considers such methods as these "positively injurious"; he prefers to give the learner a thousand and one isolated facts, and carefully to withhold every clue by which they may be grouped, classified and remembered. The method followed in this work is more or less novel, being a compromise between Sievers and Sweet, an attempt to hit the happy mean; for, while the basis of arrangement has been the practical convenience of the learner in studying the actually existing phenomena of the language, no pains have been spared in order that he may have nothing to unlearn in the further pursuit of the subject. Some empirical rules are given, but they are of a quiet, harmless sort; Germanic has been taken as a guide throughout, although it is not needlessly obtruded. A few difficulties have necessarily been deferred to a later stage. It would have given a specious air of completeness to the book to have added a section dealing with Old English syntax; but I am strongly of opinion that for the present such aid is best given in notes on selected texts. For the rest, it is unnecessary to enlarge on the methods of exposition here devised or adopted, or to make the reviewer's task easy by calling attention to the principal innovations. The ultimate appeal as to the arrangement, the methods, the necessity, and the utility of the work will be to the experience of readers and students; and their counsel and co-operation are cordially asked, for its correction and improvement.

My obligations to Sweet are a part of our national debt to him as a pioneer in English philology. My indebtedness to Sievers is obvious and well-nigh inestimable. I have made abundant use of Cosijn's *Altwestsächsische Grammatik*, an incomparable storehouse of examples. My warmest thanks are hereby tendered to Prof. Napier, whose timely advice and assistance have often encouraged me in the studies of which this book is the outcome; to a lady, whose name I am not permitted to mention, for reading the proof-sheets with equal acumen and care; to Mr B. J. Hayes, M.A., of St John's College, for giving me the benefit of his great experience in all that is meant by "seeing through the press"; and to the officials of the University Press, who have spared neither trouble nor expense in meeting my wishes, for example in banishing (I hope for ever) the italic digraph *œ*, indistinguishable from *ce*, and having the elegant character æ specially cast for this book.

A. J. W.

CAMBRIDGE,
    *March*, 1897.

# CONTENTS.

|      |                                          | PAGE |
| ---- | ---------------------------------------- | ---- |
|      | PARADIGMS . . . . | 1 |

## PART I. INFLECTION.

| SECT. |                                                    |      |
| ----- | -------------------------------------------------- | ---- |
| 1.    | INTRODUCTORY . . . . . . . . . | 9 |
| 3.    | ALPHABET AND PRONUNCIATION . . . . . | 11 |
| 6.    | NOUNS . . . . . . . . . . . | 14 |
| 16.   | I. Strong Nouns . . . . . | 20 |
| 16.   | A. Ordinary Declension . . . . | ib. |
| 16.   | 1. Masculines . . . . . . | ib. |
| 20.   | 2. Neuters . . . . . . | 22 |
| 26.   | 3. Feminines . . . . . . | 25 |
| 31.   | (i) *W*-Stems (*all genders*) . . | 28 |
| 33.   | (ii) *J*-Stems ,, ,, . . | 30 |
| 34.   | (iii) *I*-Stems ,, ,, . . | 31 |
| 36.   | B. Minor Declensions . . . . | 34 |
| 36.   | 4. *U*-Stems . . . . . . | ib. |
| 37.   | 5. *R*-Stems . . . . . . | 35 |
| 38.   | 6. *ND*-Stems . . . . . . | 36 |
| 39.   | 7. Other Stems . . . . . . | ib. |
| 40.   | II. Weak Nouns . . . . . | 38 |
| 41.   | ADJECTIVES . . . . . . . . | 39 |
| 42.   | Strong Declension . . . . . | 40 |
| 47.   | Weak Declension . . . . . . | 45 |
| 48.   | Participles . . . . . . . | 46 |

| SECT. | | | PAGE |
|---|---|---|---|
| 50. | COMPARISON | | 47 |
| 50. | I. Adjectives | | ib. |
| 52. | II. Adverbs | | 50 |
| 54. | NUMERALS | | 51 |
| 56. | PRONOUNS | | 54 |
| 56. | I. Personal | | ib. |
| 57. | II. Reflexive | | 55 |
| 58. | III. Possessive (Adjectives) | | 56 |
| 59. | IV. Demonstrative | | 57 |
| 60. | V. Relative | | 58 |
| 61. | VI. Interrogative | | ib. |
| 62. | VII. Indefinite | | 59 |
| 63. | VERBS | | 60 |
| 64. | | Strong and Weak | ib. |
| 66. | I. | Strong Verbs | 63 |
| 68. | | 2nd and 3rd Singular Present | 65 |
| 70. | | Gradation | 68 |
| 72. | | Classes of Strong Verbs | 71 |
| 80. | | Weak Presents | 82 |
| 81. | | Contracted Verbs | 85 |
| 82. | II. | Weak Verbs | 89 |
| 83. | | Class I ("Wean-Ween") | 90 |
| 90. | | ,, II ("Tell") | 97 |
| 91. | | ,, III ("Look") | 100 |
| 93. | | ,, IV: Mixed Verbs | 102 |
| 95. | III. | Past-Present Verbs | 104 |
| 96. | IV. | Anomalous Verbs | 108 |

## PART II. PHONOLOGY.

| | | | |
|---|---|---|---|
| 98. | STRESSED VOWELS (and Diphthongs) | | 112 |
| 98. | A. Downward History.—OE. Primary Vowels | | ib. |
| 113. | | Table of Correspondences | 113 |
| 114. | B. The Old English Sound-laws | | 119 |
| 117. | | Mutation | 121 |
| 118. | | I. *I*-Mutation | 122 |
| 131. | | II. *U*-Mutation | 127 |
| 135. | | III. Palatal Mutation | 129 |

## CONTENTS.

| SECT. | | | PAGE |
|---|---|---|---|
| 139. | IV. | Breaking | 130 |
| 140. | V. | Glide-Diphthongisation | 132 |
| 141. | VI. | Palatal Diphthongisation | ib. |
| 145. | VII. | ,,  Monophthongisation | 134 |
| 146. | VIII. | Influence of Preceding W | 135 |
| 147. | IX. | ,,   ,, Following W | 136 |
| 148. | X. | ,,   ,,   ,, Nasal | ib. |
| 153. | XI. | Loss of Nasal | 138 |
| 154. | XII. | Contraction (and Absorption) | ib. |
| 159. | XIII. | Loss of G and H | 141 |
| 161. | XIV. | Lengthening | 142 |
| 162. | XV. | Shortening | ib. |
| 163. | C. | Upward History.—Selected Examples | ib. |
| 164. | CONSONANTS | | 149 |
| 165. | I. | Loss | ib. |
| 166. | II. | Assimilation | 150 |
| 167. | III. | Metathesis | ib. |
| 168. | IV. | Gemination | ib. |
| 169. | V. | Verner's Law | 151 |

### APPENDIX.—WORD-FORMATION.

| 170. | I. | Formation of Adverbs | 153 |
|---|---|---|---|
| 174. | II. | Prefixes | 155 |
| 175. | III. | Suffixes | 158 |

## ABBREVIATIONS, ETC.

OE. Old English.
EWS. Early West Saxon.
LWS. Late West Saxon.
> becomes, became, becoming, passes into, etc.
< (is) derived from, etc.
<< alternating with.

TO

C. W.

# PARADIGMS.

Some such plan of work as the following is recommended to the beginner. (1) Study the paradigms given below. (2) By their aid work your way through the earlier extracts, or the whole, of the companion *Reading Primer*. (3) Continue your reading side by side with the systematic study of the large print of, first the Accidence, then the Phonology. (4) Work carefully through the whole book again, small and large print, making all the cross references.

## STRONG NOUNS.

|  | Masc. | Neut. | | Fem. | |
|---|---|---|---|---|---|
|  |  | *Singular.* | | | |
| Nom. | stān, *stone* | scip, *ship* | word, *word* | giefu[1], *gift* | lār[1], *lore* |
| Acc. | stān | scip | word | giefe | lāre |
| Gen. | stānes | scipes | wordes | giefe | lāre |
| Dat. | stāne | scipe | worde | giefe | lāre |
|  |  | *Plural.* | | | |
| N. Acc. | stānas | scipu[1] | word[1] | giefa, -e | lāra, -e |
| Gen. | stāna | scipa | worda | giefa | lāra |
| Dat. | stānum | scipum | wordum | giefum | lāru |

[1] See § 9.

W.

## WEAK NOUNS.

|  | Masc. | Neut. | Fem. |
|---|---|---|---|
|  |  | *Singular.* |  |
| *Nom.* | guma, *man* | eáge, *eye* | heorte, *heart* |
| *Acc.* | guman | eáge | heortan |
| *Gen.* | guman | eágan | heortan |
| *Dat.* | guman | eágan | heortan |
|  |  | *Plural.* |  |
| *N. Acc.* | guman | eágan | heortan |
| *Gen.* | gumena | eágena | heortena |
| *Dat.* | gumum | eágum | heortum |

## ADJECTIVES.

### I. Strong Form.

|  | Masc. | Neut. |  | Fem. |  |
|---|---|---|---|---|---|
|  |  | *Singular.* |  |  |  |
| *Nom.* | til, *good* gōd, *good* | til | gōd | tilu[1] | gōd[1] |
| *Acc.* | tilne gōdne | til | gōd | tile | gōde |
| *Gen.* | tiles gōdes |  |  | tilre | gōdre |
| *Dat.* | tilum gōdum |  |  | tilre | gōdre |
| *Instr.* | tile gōde |  |  |  |  |
|  |  | *Plural.* |  |  |  |
| *N. Acc.* | tile  gōde | tilu[1] | gōd[1] | tila,-e | gōda,-e |
| *Gen.* |  | tilra | gōdra |  |  |
| *Dat.* |  | tilum | gōdum |  |  |

[1] See § 9.

## ADJECTIVES (*continued*)

II. WEAK FORM (*after demonstratives*).

|  | Masc. | Neut. | Fem. | | Plural. |
|---|---|---|---|---|---|
|  | *Singular.* | | | | |
| Nom. | gōda | gōde | gōde | } | gōdan |
| Acc. | gōdan | gōde | gōdan | | |
| Gen. | | gōdan | | | gōdra |
| Dat. | | gōdan | | | gōdum |

## PRONOUNS.

### "I"

|  | *Sing.* | *Dual.* | *Plural.* |
|---|---|---|---|
| Nom. | ic | wit | wē |
| Acc. | mē | unc | ūs |
| Gen. | mīn | uncer | ūre |
| Dat. | mē | unc | ūs |

### "Thou"

|  | *Sing.* | *Dual.* | *Plural.* |
|---|---|---|---|
| Nom. | ðū | git | gē |
| Acc. | ðē | inc | ēow |
| Gen. | ðīn | incer | ēower |
| Dat. | ðē | inc | ēow |

### "He"  "It"  "She"  "They"

|  | Masc. | Neut. | Fem. | | Plural. |
|---|---|---|---|---|---|
|  | *Singular.* | | | | |
| Nom. | hē | hit | hēo | } | hīe |
| Acc. | hine | hit | hīe | | |
| Gen. | his | | hiere | | hiera |
| Dat. | him | | hiere | | him |

## PRONOUNS (*continued*).

### "The," "that."

|  | Masc. | Neut. | Fem. |  |
|---|---|---|---|---|
|  | *Singular.* |  |  | *Plural.* |
| *Nom.* | sē | ðæt | sēo | ðā |
| *Acc.* | ðone | ðæt | ðā | |
| *Gen.* | ðæs |  | ðǣre | ðāra |
| *Dat.* | ðǣm |  | ðǣre | ðǣm |
| *Instr.* | ðȳ |  |  |  |

### "This"

|  | *Singular.* |  |  | *Plural.* |
|---|---|---|---|---|
| *Nom.* | ðes | ðis | ðēos | ðās |
| *Acc.* | ðisne | ðis | ðās | |
| *Gen.* | ðisses |  | ðisse | ðissa |
| *Dat.* | ðissum |  | ðisse | ðissum |
| *Instr.* | ðȳs |  |  |  |

### "Who?"  "What?"

|  | Masc. | Neut. |
|---|---|---|
|  | *Singular.* |  |
| *Nom.* | hwā | hwæt |
| *Acc.* | hwone | hwæt |
| *Gen.* | hwæs |  |
| *Dat.* | hwǣm |  |
| *Instr.* | hwȳ |  |

# VERBS.

## I. Strong.

|  | Present | Past |
|---|---|---|

*Indicative.*

| Sing. 1. | helpe, *help* | healp |
|---|---|---|
| 2. | hilpst | hulpe |
| 3. | hilpð | healp |
| Plur. | helpað | hulpon |

*Subjunctive.*

| Sing. | helpe | hulpe |
|---|---|---|
| Plur. | helpen | hulpen |

*Imperative.*

help (*sg.*), helpað (*pl.*)

*Infinitive.*

helpan, *dat.* tō helpanne

*Participles.*

helpende          geholpen

## Principal Parts of Strong Verbs.

| Class | Infin. | 3rd Sing. | Past Sing. | Past Pl. | Past Part. |
|---|---|---|---|---|---|
| I. | scīnan, *shine* | scīnð | scān | scinon | scinen |
| II. | crēopan, *creep* | crīepð | crēap | crupon | cropen |
| IIIa. | helpan, *help* | hilpð | healp | hulpon | holpen |
| IIIb. | drincan, *drink* | drincð | dronc | druncon | druncen |
| IV. | beran, *bear* | birð | bær | bǣron | boren |
| V. | tredan, *tread* | tritt | træd | trǣdon | treden |
| VI. | faran, *fare* | færð | fōr | fōron | faren |

## VERBS (*continued*).

### II. WEAK.

(1) *-an* Verb.   (2) *-ian* Verb.

#### PRESENT *Indicative.*

| | | | |
|---|---|---|---|
| *Sing.* | 1. | dēme, *judge* | lōcie, *look* |
| | 2. | dēm(e)st | lōcast |
| | 3. | dēm(e)ð | lōcað |
| *Plur.* | | dēmað | lōciað |

#### PRESENT *Subjunctive.*

| | | |
|---|---|---|
| *Sing.* | dēme | lōcie |
| *Plur.* | dēmen | lōcien |

#### PAST *Indicative.*

| | | | |
|---|---|---|---|
| *Sing.* | 1. | dēmde | lōcode |
| | 2. | dēmdest | lōcodest |
| | 3. | dēmde | lōcode |
| *Plur.* | | dēmdon | lōcedon |

#### PAST *Subjunctive.*

| | | |
|---|---|---|
| *Sing.* | dēmde | lōcode |
| *Plur.* | dēmden | lōcoden |

#### *Imperative.*

| | | |
|---|---|---|
| *Sing.* | dēm | lōca |
| *Plur.* | dēmað | lōciað |

#### *Infinitive.*

| | |
|---|---|
| dēman | lōcian |

#### *Participles.*

| | | |
|---|---|---|
| *Pres.* | dēmende | lōciende |
| *Past.* | gedēmed | gelōcod |

## VERBS (*continued*).

### III. "To be."

|  | Present |  | Past |
|---|---|---|---|
| *Indicative.* | | | |
| *Sing.* 1. | eom | bēo | wæs |
| 2. | eart | bist | wǣre |
| 3. | is | bið | wæs |
| *Plur.* | sind(on) | bēoð | wǣron |
| *Subjunctive.* | | | |
| *Sing.* | sīe | bēo | wǣre |
| *Plur.* | sīen | bēon | wǣren |

*Imperative.*

wes, wesað bēo, bēoð

*Infinitive.*

wesan bēon

*Participles.*

wesende bēonde *wanting*

# ELEMENTARY OLD ENGLISH GRAMMAR.

## PART I. INFLECTION.

### Introductory.

1. The position of Old English in the family of languages to which it belongs can best be shown by means of a genealogical table:

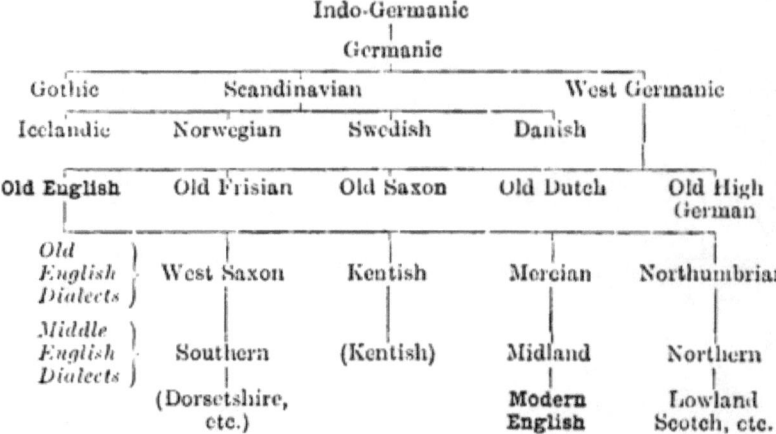

The **dialects** of Old English are thus seen to be four, of which the most important is West Saxon, because almost the whole of the extant remains of Old English literature has come down to us in that dialect. It is not the direct parent, but rather, as it were, the uncle, of Modern English, in tracing the ancestry of which through West Saxon we therefore deflect from the straight line of descent. But this disadvantage is compensated by the ampleness of West Saxon materials in comparison with the meagreness of the remains of Old Mercian. Northumbria and Mercia were peopled principally by Angles: hence 'Anglian' is often used as a common name for the Northumbrian and Mercian dialects, which were in many respects similar.

Old English literature belongs chiefly to two periods: the Northumbrian period, in the 7th and 8th centuries, to which belong nearly all the great monuments of Old English poetry; and the West Saxon period, from the 9th to the 11th century, the classical period of Old English prose. But, although the best of our early poetry was composed in Northumbrian, it must be remembered that it has been handed down to us in West Saxon transcriptions, containing however not infrequent traces of its origin in the retention of Anglian forms of words.

2. Old English was the language spoken by the Teutonic inhabitants of England before the Conquest (and for a short time after). In the title of this book the name "Old English" has been used, for convenience' sake, as synonymous with "(Early) **West Saxon** dialect." West Saxon before about the year 900 A.D., or the close of Alfred's reign, is known as Early West Saxon; after about 950 A.D. it is called Late West Saxon. Late West Saxon shows numerous signs of inflectional decay, especially in the assimilation of inflections, before the Norman Conquest. Early West Saxon is therefore the purest form of Old English of which sufficient remains for grammatical study are extant. From an elementary text-book such as this the other dialects are almost entirely excluded, as beyond its aim and scope. Strictly speaking, then, Old English is the collective name for the Teutonic dialects spoken in England before the Conquest; but it is often conveniently used as the name for the earlier and purer form of the classical West Saxon.

The chief distinguishing **marks of** the various Old English **dialects** are these:

(1) **West Saxon** represents Germanic $\bar{æ}$ (West Germanic $\bar{a}$) by $\bar{æ}$, the other dialects by $\bar{e}$; it accurately discriminates *ea* and *eo*; it lost the sound of *œ* early; it replaces the *-u*, *-o*, of the first person singular present indicative by *-e*. The distinguishing mark of **Early West Saxon** is that the *i*-mutation of *ea* and *eo* is *ie*, and that of *ēa* and *ēo* is *īe*, passing into **Late West Saxon** *i* or *y*, and *ī* or *ȳ*, respectively. Some special forms and inflections peculiar to Late West Saxon will be found in the paragraphs of this grammar.

(2) **Northumbrian** (from which Mercian does not greatly differ) drops final *n*; frequently terminates the 3rd person singular and the whole of the plural present indicative in *s*, instead of ð; confuses *ea* and *eo* (short and long); has a liking for the *œ* sound (short and long); and has its inflections unsettled earlier than the other dialects.

(3) **Kentish** prefers *ia*, *io* to *ea*, *eo*; vocalises *g* into *i* (e.g. *dæi* for *dæg*); and substitutes *e* for *y*.

## Alphabet and Pronunciation.

3. The Old English alphabet consisted of the following characters: **a, æ, b, c, d, e, f, g, h, i, (k,) l, m, n, o, p, r, s, t, þ, ð, u, ƿ (= w), x, y.** k is occasionally found for **c**. This alphabet is both defective and redundant.

(1) It is **redundant** in the letter *x*, which stands for *cs* (*ks*) or *hs*.

(2) It is **defective** in having no special symbol for: (*a*) the sound of the semi-vowel *j*, which is represented sometimes by *i*, much oftener by *g*; (*b*) the sound of short *open* $e^1$ (printed *ę* in this book), and the sound of short *open* $o^1$ (printed *ǫ* in this book); (*c*) the voiced (sonant, flat, soft) sounds corresponding to *f*, *s*, þ, i.e. the sounds usually represented in modern English by *v*, *z*, *th* in *thine* (= dh). Moreover, *c*, *g*, *sc* and *h* represent both guttural and palatal sounds.

---

[1] Modern English has only the open sounds of short *e* and short *o*. See § 4.

N.B. **I-mutation**[1] **and Breaking.**

(1) The vowels produced by *i*-mutation are *i*, **ę** (æ), **ǣ**, **ie**, **īe**, **ȳ**, **y**, **ȳ**, of which those printed **black** are in every instance in EWS. (with unimportant exceptions) produced by *i*-mutation.

(2) Breaking includes the change of *a* to *ea* and *e* to *eo* before *r* + consonant, *l* + consonant, *h* + consonant, or *h* final.

Full details are given in Part II.

4. **Pronunciation.**—N.B. *Every letter in Old English must be fully sounded, whatever its position.*

The **vowels** *a, e, i, o, u* in Old English had what may be called their "continental," or Italian, sound.

| | | | |
|---|---|---|---|
| a | = *the* a *in* | answer[2], *only shorter.* |
| ā | = | a | father |
| æ | = | a | man |
| ǣ | = | a | care |
| e (close) | = | é | *Fr.* épais. |
| ę (open) | = | e | men |
| ē | = | ey | they |
| i | = | i | pin |
| ī | = | i | machine |
| o (close) | = | o | *Ger.* Gott |
| ǫ (open) | = | o | not |
| ō | = | o | note |
| u | = | u | put |
| ū | = | u | rule |
| y | = | u | *Ger.* hübsch, *Fr.* ultérieur |
| ȳ | = | u | *Ger.* grün, *Fr.* voiture. |

If the values of *e, o, y, ȳ*, assigned above cause much difficulty the values of *ę, ǫ, i, ī*, may be substituted for them for a time.

[1] "Mutation" and "mutated" are frequently used in the following pages with reference to *i*-mutation only.
[2] Not of course in the affected pronunciation of the "finishing" schoolmistress and her tribe: 'Anne-Sir.'

The **diphthongs** of Old English are *ea, eo (io), ie*, short and long. The stress falls on the first element, which in *ea* is the open sound, and in *eo* the close sound, of *e*.

The pronunciation of the **consonants** *b, d, k, l, m, n, p, r, t, w, x*, does not differ materially from that of modern English.

    c = mod. *k*
    g =   *y* in *get*.

These two letters (and *h*), as has been said, had both a guttural and a palatal sound, and *g* was also both a spirant and a stop. But, as it is hardly possible for the beginner to decide for himself which sound they had in a particular word, it seems best, at least at this stage, to adopt one value for each letter (a practice which some eminent scholars never depart from, except for phonetic exposition)[1].

N.B. cg = gg (< gj): ex. *lecgan*, to lay.

**h**, (1) initial, is a mere aspirate, as in English *hard*: exs. *hē*, he; *hlūd*, loud; (2) medial and final, is a voiceless spirant, like the *ch* in Scotch *loch* (guttural), or the *ch* in Ger. *ich* (palatal): exs. *hēah*, high; *niht*, night.

**f, s, þ, ð** are (1) *voiceless* (surd, sharp, hard) whenever possible, i.e. always when initial, always when final, and when medial in voiceless company (i.e. in company with another voiceless consonant): exs. *fōd*, food; *hors*, horse; *siððan*, since; (2) *voiced* when medial between voiced sounds (vowels, liquids, nasals, voiced consonants): exs. *ofer*, over; *hālsian*, to greet; *wiðinnan*, within.

It would be convenient to appropriate þ for the voiceless sound, *th* in *thin*, and ð for the voiced sound, *dh* in *thine*, as in Icelandic; but Old

---

[1] The author is confirmed in this opinion by the hopeless confusion that results from the attempt to expound this matter fully in what are professedly elementary text-books. Sievers comes to the conclusion that Old English *g* was most frequently a voiced spirant, but his proofs seem inconclusive for initial *g*. In any case, the voiced spirant *g* is a sound not only foreign to modern English, but one difficult for English people to acquire. To say, as is usually done, that it is the sound of *g* in Ger. *sagen*, is to ignore that the *g* in *sagen*, on the stage and in North Germany generally, is a voiced stop.

English MSS. afford no justification for this usage. In printing texts it is usual to follow the MSS. exactly. Throughout this book the sign ð is alone used; it came into use much earlier than þ, and is found almost exclusively in the best of the older MSS.

**5. Stress.**—The chief stress, or syllabic accent, usually falls on the *first syllable* of Old English words: ex. *hláford*, lord.

**Exceptions.** (1) In derivative verbs, the principal stress falls almost invariably on the root, not on the prefix: ex. *arísan*, to arise.

(2) In nouns and adjectives compounded with *ge-*, *be-* and sometimes *for-*, the chief stress falls on the radical syllable, not on the prefix; but in the case of other prefixes, the stress falls on the prefix: exs. *geféra*, companion; *behát*, promise; but *ǫ́ndlēan*, requital.

## NOUNS.

**6. Gender.**—The modern English system of gender is unknown to Old English, in which the names of things are masculine, feminine or neuter. There are two ways which enable us to determine the gender of many nouns.

(1) By *meaning*. Names of males are masculine; names of females are feminine; names of young creatures (because their sex is less easily distinguishable) are neuter: exs. *se cyning*, the king; *sēo cwēn*, the queen; *ðæt cild*, *bearn*, the child. **Exceptions**: *ðæt wíf*, the woman; *ðæt mægden*, the girl.

(2) By *termination*. (*a*) Nouns ending in *-a*, *-að*, *-els*, *-end*, *-ere*, *-dōm*, *-hád*, *-scipe*, *-stafas*, names of persons in *-ing* and *-ling*, and compounds ending with a masculine word, are masculine. (*b*) Nouns ending in *-estre*, *-nes*, *-rǣden*, *-ð* (except *-að*), *-ung* (*-ing*), and compounds ending with a feminine word, are feminine. (*c*) Nouns ending in *-ern*, *-rīce*, *-lác*, and compounds ending with a neuter word, are neuter.

**7. Cases.**—Old English has the following cases: Nominative, Accusative, Genitive, Dative, Instrumental. The Nominative serves also as a Vocative. The Instrumental in *nouns* never differs in form from the Dative, and it is therefore omitted in the noun paradigms.

**8. Strong and Weak.**—Every noun in Old English belongs to either the strong or the weak declension; a few have both strong and weak forms: as, *monn, monna*, man. (On the other hand, almost all adjectives may be declined both strong and weak: see § 41.)

A glance at the paradigms will show that it is easy **to distinguish weak** nouns and adjectives **from strong**, except in the nom. sing. and dat. plural. All weak nouns end in a vowel in the nom. sing.:

(1) All nouns ending in **-a** are weak masculines.

(2) Weak fems. and neuters end in *-e*, all but a few short-stemmed fems. in *-u*. But by no means all nouns ending in *-e* or *-u* are weak.

**9. Loss of final e and u.**—The simple practical rule is this (great attention should be paid to it, for it covers a large number of instances): *Final* **e** (earlier *i*) *and* **u** *are generally retained after a short syllable, dropped after a long syllable*[1]. The applications of this rule are numerous and important.

(1) Original short *i*-stems retain final *-e*, while long stems drop it: cp. *wine*, friend, *spere*, spear, with *giest*, stranger, *bēn*, boon.

(2) **The nom. sing. of fem. nouns and the nom. plur. of neuter nouns of the ordinary declension retain final -u after a short syllable, drop it after a long syllable.** Cp. *giefu*, gift, with *sprǣc*, speech; and *scipu*, ships, with *hūs*, houses. Cp. also the modern plurals *deer, sheep, swine*.

---

[1] A syllable is long if it has a long vowel or if it ends in two consonants.

(3) **Exactly the same rule applies to the fem. sing. and neuter plural of adjs.**: cp. fem. sing. and neut. pl. *tilu*, useful, with *gōd*, good.

(4) **The same rule applies to disyllabic nouns and adjs.: -u is generally retained after a short second (or even third) syllable.** Exs.: *rīce*, realm, pl. *rīcu*; *hēafod*, head, pl. *hēaf(o)du*; *grēne*, green, fem. sing. and neut. pl. *grēnu*; *æðele*, noble, *æðelu*.

Exceptions. (*a*) After *two short* syllables there is a good deal of irregularity. Thus *firen* (fem.), crime, has no final *u*; the fem. sing. and neut. pl. of *micel*, great, and *monig*, many, are *micel*, *monig*, but also *mic(e)lu*, *monigu*; the pls. of *mægen* and *wæter* are *mægenu*, *wæt(e)ru*.

(*b*) Late West Saxon texts not only break the rules of this and the next section, but show almost every possible grammatical irregularity. For this reason only the more frequent and important variations of Late West Saxon from Early West Saxon will be noticed in this book.

**10. Loss of middle vowels.**—Some disyllabic nouns and adjectives with a short second syllable, such as *ēðel*, native land, *dēofol*, devil, *ōðer*, second, syncopate the middle vowel in inflection according to the following

*Rule*: **When a termination beginning with a vowel is added to a disyllable, whose first syllable is long and second syllable short, the vowel of the second syllable is usually dropped.** Thus:

| | | | |
|---|---|---|---|
| *ēðel*, native land, | long + short, | gen. *ēðles*, | not *ēðeles*. |
| *lȳtel*, little, | long + short, | gen. *lȳtles*, | not *lȳteles*. |
| *heofon*, heaven, | short + short, | gen. *heofones*, | not *heofnes*. |
| *hærfest*, autumn, | long + long, | gen. *hærfæstes*, | not *hærfstes*. |

N.B. It is obvious that the above rule cannot apply when the flectional syllable begins with a consonant. Thus we have acc. masc. sing. *ōðerne*, gen. pl. *lȳtelra*.

Exceptions. (*a*) *Micel*, great, *yfel*, evil (both short + short), syncopate the middle vowel in inflection: thus, gen. *micles*, *yfles*, dat. *miclum*, pl. *yf(e)lu* (see below).

(b) When the above rule and that given in § 9. 4 both apply to the same word, the above rule may or may not be observed: thus we find nom. pls. hēaf(o)du, dēoflu, earfoðu, bismru, id(e)lu (neut.).

**11. Intrusive vowels.**—Old English words ending in consonant + vocalic liquid or nasal often introduced a vowel before the liquid or nasal, making the latter into a distinct syllable, as in *fugol*, bird (Gothic *fugls*). This intrusive vowel was usually *e* when the preceding vowel was palatal, most often *o* when the preceding vowel was guttural[1]: exs. æcer, field; bēacen, beacon; ātor, poison. These words for the most part conform to the rule laid down in § 10: thus we have gen. *wintres* from *winter* (long + short), but *fægeres* from *fæger* (short + short).

Exception: *fugol*, bird, gen. *fugles*, pl. *fuglas*.

In the following words the second vowel is intrusive:

| æppel, *apple* | tāc(e)n, *token* | fōdor, *fodder* |
| tempel, *temple* | wǣp(e)n, *weapon* | hlūtor, *pure* |
| māðum, *treasure* | ceaster, *city* | hungor, *hunger* |
| bēacen, *beacon* | clūstor, *prison* | wundor, *marvel* |
| fāc(e)n, *treachery* | finger, *finger* | etc. |

**12. Variation of middle vowels.**—The *o* or *u* of the second syllable of a word tends to become *e* whenever a third (flexional) syllable containing a *guttural* vowel is added. This law is well illustrated by the declension of such a noun as *heofon*:

| Sing. | Nom. heofon | Gen. heofones | Dat. heofone |
| Plur. | | heofenas | heofena | heofenum. |

Similarly we find *staðol*, pillar, gen. *staðoles*; but pl. *staðelas*, and the verb *staðelian* (*i* < *ō*), to found. Cp. also the past sing. *lōcode* with the past pl. *lōcedon*.

The explanation of this change is to be sought partly in the weakening of the stress on the second syllable, partly in a tendency to alternate palatal and guttural vowels which has been called "secondary gradation."

---

[1] *a, o, u* are guttural vowels, all others are palatal.

## 13. Loss of consonants.

(1) *Loss of medial* h. When a final *h* becomes medial in inflection it is dropped.

   (a) If between liquid and vowel, there is compensatory lengthening of the preceding vowel: exs. *mearh*, horse, gen. *mēares*, pl. *mēaras*: *holh*, hole, gen. *hōles*, &c.; cp. *fēolan*, penetrate, < *fēolhan*.

   (b) If between vowel and vowel, contraction (see § 154) results: ex. *scōh*, shoe, pl. *scōs*; *eoh*, horse, gen. *ēos*.

(2) *Simplification of final double consonant*. The simplification of a double final consonant is usual in Old English, whether the geminate was original or arose from earlier consonant + *j*[1]. Yet the etymological spelling is also not infrequent.

Thus we have:

(a) in the ordinary masc. declension (§ 16),

| Nom. | Gen. | Pl. |
|---|---|---|
| weal(l), wall | wealles | weallas, etc. |
| dyn(n), din | dynnes | dynnas |

(b) in the ordinary neuter declension (§ 20),

| | | |
|---|---|---|
| ful(l), cup | fulles | ful(l) |
| cyn(n), race | cynnes | cyn(n) |

(c) in the ordinary fem. declension (§ 26),

| | | |
|---|---|---|
| heal(l), hall | healle | healla,-e |
| ben(n), wound | benne | benna,-e |

and similarly

| | |
|---|---|
| hen(n), *hen* | sib(b), *kinship* |
| nyt(t), *profit* | syn(n), *sin*. |

(d) The same thing is seen in adjs. (§ 43), in the imperative sing. of verbs (e.g. *gecier* from *gecierran*), and elsewhere.

**Exception.** Final *cg* (=*gg*) is never simplified: *secg*, man; *hrycg*, back.

---

[1] Double consonant < consonant + *j* can usually be known by the preceding mutated vowel. In West Germanic, every consonant (except r) doubled before j after a short vowel (see § 168).

**14. Endings.**—The following table gives the commonest endings in the declensions of **strong** masc., fem., and neuter nouns respectively:

|  | Masc. | Neut. | Fem. |
|---|---|---|---|
|  |  | *Singular.* |  |
| *Nom.* |  |  | (u) |
| *Acc.* |  |  | e |
| *Gen.* |  | es | e |
| *Dat.* |  | e | e |
|  |  | *Plural.* |  |
| *N. Acc.* | as | (u) | a (e) |
| *Gen.* |  | a |  |
| *Dat.* |  | um |  |

Notes. (1) The **gen. pl.** of strong nouns invariably ends in **-a** (rarely -*na*); of weak nouns in **-ena**; of all adjs. in **-ra**.

(2) The **dat. pl.** of all nouns and adjs. ends in **-um** (other forms of which are -*un*, -*on*, -*an*).

**15. Declensions.**—The declensions of OE. nouns are arranged as follows for the sake of simplicity and convenience:

I. Strong Nouns:
    Ordinary Declension:    1. Masculines.
                                  2. Neuters.
                                  3. Feminines.
                                               (i) *W*-stems.
                                               (ii) *J*-stems.
                                               (iii) *I*-stems.
    Minor Declensions:    4. *U*-stems.
                                  5. *R*-stems.
                                  6. *ND*-stems.
                                  7. Other stems.

II. Weak Nouns.

## DECLENSIONS.

### I. STRONG NOUNS.

*ORDINARY DECLENSION*[1].—1. **MASCULINES.**

**16. Primary paradigms**: *stān*, stone; *hierde*, (shep)herd.

*Singular.*

| | | |
|---|---|---|
| *N. Acc.* | stān | hierde |
| *Gen.* | stānes | hierdes |
| *Dat.* | stāne | hierde |

*Plural.*

| | | |
|---|---|---|
| *N. Acc.* | stānas | hierdas |
| *Gen.* | stāna | hierda |
| *Dat.* | stānum | hierdum |

Notes. (1) *Stān* is an original *o*-stem (i.e. corresponds to the Latin and Greek *o*-declensions), *hierde* an original *jo*- stem (see § 33). There is no difference in inflections (final -*e* is invariably elided before a termination beginning with a vowel); but traces of the original *j* of *hierde* are seen in the final -*e* and in the mutated vowel of the root.

(2) **Locatives**, without inflection, are seen in

| | |
|---|---|
| tō-dæg, *to-day* | ælce dæg, *each day* |
| tō-morgen, *to-morrow* | æt hām, *at home* |
| tō, *from his āgnum hām, to, from his own home* | |

---

[1] The arrangement of declensions here adopted is a compromise between a complete ignoring of the original stems, which are often obscured beyond recognition in Old English—a method which has the disadvantage of not leading on and up to the study of cognate and earlier languages; and, on the other hand, an undue multiplication of declensions (according to stems), which in Old English sometimes differ only in a single case or form. *W*-stems, *j*-stems and *i*-stems, which differ in *inflection* from the ordinary declension, are given in §§ 32—34; all the rest are included here.

(3) Sǣ (Gothic *saiws*), sea, is both masc. and fem.:

|  | Singular. | Plural. |
|---|---|---|
| N. Acc. | sǣ | sǣs, sǣ |
| Gen. | sǣs, sǣ, sǣwe | sǣwa |
| Dat. | sǣ, sǣwe | sǣ(u)m, sǣwum |

### 17. Secondary Paradigm.

*Dæg*, day, returns to the original root-vowel in the plural (as explained in Part II., § 100).

|  | Sing. | Plural. |
|---|---|---|
| N. Acc. | dæg | dagas |
| Gen. | dæges | daga |
| Dat. | dæge | dagum |

NOTES. (1) In the same way are declined

hwæl, *whale*   pæð, *path*
stæf, *staff*

(2) *Mǣg*, kinsman, with a long vowel, is similarly declined (see § 105), but the vowel of the singular sometimes invades the plural:

|  | Sing. | Plural. |
|---|---|---|
| N. Acc. | mǣg | māgas, mǣgas |
| Gen. | mǣges | māga |
| Dat. | mǣge | māgum, mǣgum |

### 18. Secondary Paradigm.

*Brīdel*, bridle, will serve as a model of the syncopated declension, the rule for which is given in § 10:

|  | Sing. | Plural. |
|---|---|---|
| N. Acc. | brīdel | brīdlas |
| Gen. | brīdles | brīdla |
| Dat. | brīdle | brīdlum |

In the same way are declined all disyllabic masculines with the first syllable long and the second short.

**19. Secondary Paradigm.** *Mearh*, horse (see § 13):

|  | *Sing.* | *Plural.* |
|---|---|---|
| N. Acc. | mearh | mēaras |
| Gen. | mēares | mēara |
| Dat. | mēare | mēarum |

Decline in the same way *fearh*, swine; *seolh*, seal; *Wealh*, Welshman, foreigner.

## ORDINARY DECLENSION.—2. **NEUTERS.**

**20. Primary paradigms:**

(*a*) Long monosyllable: *word*, word.
(*b*) Short   ,,   : *hof*, dwelling.
(*c*) Disyllables   : *wīte*, punishment; *sife*, sieve.

*Singular.*

|  |  |  |  |  |
|---|---|---|---|---|
| N. Acc. | word | hof | wīte | sife |
| Gen. | wordes | hofes | wītes | sifes |
| Dat. | worde | hofe | wīte | sife |

*Plural.*

|  |  |  |  |  |
|---|---|---|---|---|
| N. Acc. | **word** (§ 9. 2) | **hofu** (§ 9. 2) | **wītu** (§ 9. 4) | **sifu** (§ 9. 4) |
| Gen. | worda | hofa | wīta | sifa |
| Dat. | wordum | hofum | wītum | sifum |

NOTES. (1) In deciding which paradigm a neuter noun follows, *prefixes must be ignored:* thus, *behāt*, promise, is declined like *word*.

(2) *Word* and *hof* are original neuter o-stems, *wīte* an original jo-stem (see § 33), and *sife* an original i-stem (see § 34). There is no difference in inflection; but the -*e* of the nom. sing. is a trace of the original stem of the last two words.

(3) For the -*u* of the nom. acc. plural, -*o*, -*a* are not infrequent: *witu, wito, wita*.

(1) The declension of *geat*, gate, is

|  | Singular. | Plural. |
|---|---|---|
| N. Acc. | geat (§ 143) | gatu (§ 100) |
| Gen. | geates | gata |
| Dat. | geate | gatum |

But we also find plural *geatu, geata, geatum*, where the vowel of the singular has been extended to the plural.

## 21. Secondary paradigm: *fæt*, vessel.

|  | Sing. | Plural. |
|---|---|---|
| N. Acc. | fæt (cp. § 17) | fatu (§ 100) |
| Gen. | fætes | fata |
| Dat. | fæte | fatum |

Decline in the same way

| bæð, *bath* | swæð, *track* |
|---|---|
| dæl, *dale* | træf, *tent* |

## 22. Secondary paradigm (syncopated): *hēafod*, head.

|  | Sing. | Plural. |
|---|---|---|
| N. Acc. | hēafod | hēaf(o)du (§§ 9, 10) |
| Gen. | hēafdes (§ 10) | hēafda |
| Dat. | hēafde | hēafdum |

NOTES. (1) Decline in the same way disyllabic neuters with long first and short second syllable; cp. § 18.

(2) **Exceptions.** Neuters in *-en*, like *cliewen*, ball, *nīeten*, animal, *mǣden*, maiden, where the *e* is not intrusive (as it is in *bēacen, fācen, tācen, wǣpen*, § 11), are not syncopated: gen. *nīetenes, mǣdenes*; dat. *cliewene*; pl. *nīetenu*, etc.

(3) Several neuters with intrusive vowels have two noms. plural, with and without *-u: tungol*, star, pl. *tunglu* and *tungol*; *wundor*, marvel, pl. *wundru, wundra*, and *wundor*; *wǣp(e)n*, pl. *wǣp(e)nu, wǣpeno*, and *wǣp(e)n*; *tāc(e)n*, pl. *tācnu* and *tācen*.

**23. Secondary paradigms**: *feorh*, life; *feoh*, money.

*Singular.*

| | | |
|---|---|---|
| N. Acc. | feorh | feoh |
| Gen. | fēores (§ 13) | fēos (§ 13) |
| Dat. | fēore | fēo |

*Plural.*

| | |
|---|---|
| N. Acc. | feorh |
| Gen. | fēora |
| Dat. | fēorum |

Like *feorh*, decline *holh*, hole, gen. *hōles*; like *feoh*, decline *pleoh*, danger. Cp. § 19.

**24. Secondary paradigm**: *lim*, limb.

| | *Sing.* | *Plural.* |
|---|---|---|
| N. Acc. | lim | limu, liomu (§ 132) |
| Gen. | limes | lima, lioma |
| Dat. | lime | limum, liomum |

NOTES. (1) In the same way are declined neuters with *i* or *e* before a single consonant, such as

| | |
|---|---|
| clif, *cliff* | gebed, *prayer* (*pl.* gebedu, gebeodu) |
| scip, *ship* | geset, *seat* |

(2) Plurals with *i* or *e*, *limu* etc., are most common; those with *io*, *eo*, due to *u*-mutation, decrease in frequency in later texts.

**25.** There are traces in some OE. neuters of stems corresponding to Greek neuters in **-os**, Lat. **-us, -eris** (γένος, *genus*). The *s* appears in OE. as *r*. These words are divided into two classes: (1) those which retain the *r* throughout; (2) those which retain it in the plural only.

§ 26                    STRONG NOUNS.                    25

(1) Here belong *dōgor*, day; *hrȳðer*, cattle; *salor*, hail; *sigor*, victory; *wildor*, wild beast. For the most part they follow the ordinary declension, but occasionally an uninflected dat. sing. is met with, *dōgor*, *sigor*. Plurals are *dōgor*, *hrȳðeru*, *wildru*, etc. Forms without r are also found; *sæl* as well as *salor*, *sige* and *sigor* (this word has become masculine).

(2) The words *ǣg*, egg, *cealf*, calf, and *lǫmb*, lamb, are declined alike; *cild*, child, differs somewhat.

*Singular.*

| | | |
|---|---|---|
| *N. Acc.* | cealf | cild |
| *Gen.* | cealfes | cildes |
| *Dat.* | cealfe | cilde |

*Plural.*

| | | |
|---|---|---|
| *N. Acc.* | cealfru | cild, cild(e)ru |
| *Gen.* | cealfra | cilda, cildra |
| *Dat.* | cealfrum | cildum |


*ORDINARY DECLENSION.*—3. **FEMININES**.

26. Primary paradigms:

(a) Short stem : *gi(e)fu*, gift.

(b) Long  ,,   : *stōw*, place.

*Singular.*

| | | |
|---|---|---|
| *Nom.* | **gi(e)fu, -o** | **stōw** |
| *Acc.* | gi(e)fe | stōwe |
| *Gen.* | gi(e)fe | stōwe |
| *Dat.* | gi(e)fe | stōwe |

*Plural.*

| | | |
|---|---|---|
| *N. Acc.* | gi(e)fa -e | stōwa, -e |
| *Gen.* | gi(e)fa, -ena | stōwa |
| *Dat.* | gi(e)fum | stōwum |

NOTES. (1) *Gi(e)fu* is a short *ā*-stem (corresponding to Latin and Greek *ā*-declension), *stōw* is a long *wā*-stem (see § 31). All long *ā*-stems, such as *ār*, honour, *lār*, lore, *glōf*, glove, *wund*, wound, and long *jā*-stems (see § 33), such as *gierd*, rod, yard, *wylf*, she-wolf, are declined like *stōw*. (Note the mutated root-vowels of the *jā*-stems.)

(2) The gen. pl. in -*ena* was imported from the weak declension and is found only in the later texts. It is very rarely added to long stems, never to *jā*- or *wā*-stems.

(3) In the sing. of short stems with root-vowel *a* (especially when followed by *c*), the *a* alternates with *æ* (see § 100): examples,

| | |
|---|---|
| sacu, *strife* | acc. gen. dat. sace, sæce |
| wracu, *vengeance* | wrace, wræce |

(4) Final -*o* as a variant for -*u* is so common (see § 20. 3, etc.) that it will be omitted, for the sake of simplification, in some future paradigms.

**27. Secondary paradigms**: *sāwol*, soul; *firen*, crime: to illustrate the syncopation in the first (long + short) and the absence of syncopation in the second (short + short), according to § 10.

*Singular.*

| | | |
|---|---|---|
| *Nom.* | sāwol | firen |
| *Acc.* | sāwle | firene |
| *Gen.* | sāwle | firene |
| *Dat.* | sāwle | firene |

*Plural.*

| | | |
|---|---|---|
| *N. Acc.* | sāwla, -e | firena, -e |
| *Gen.* | sāwla | firena |
| *Dat.* | sāwlum | firenum |

**28. Secondary paradigm**: *scotung*, shooting, missile.

| | *Sing.* | *Plural.* |
|---|---|---|
| *Nom.* | scotung | scotunga, -e |
| *Acc.* | scotunga, -e | scotunga, -e |
| *Gen.* | scotunga, -e | scotunga |
| *Dat.* | scotunga, -e | scotungum |

In the same way are declined all fem. abstracts in -*ung*; but those in -*ing* do not take -*a* in the singular, and so conform to the ordinary declension.

### 29. Secondary paradigm: *strengð(u)*, strength.

|  | Singular | Plural |
|---|---|---|
| Nom. | strengð, strengðu | strengða, -e, strengðu |
| Acc. | strengðe, strengðu | ,, ,, ,, |
| Gen. | ,, ,, | strengða |
| Dat. | ,, ,, | strengðum |

Two classes of feminine abstracts belong here.

(*a*) Nouns such as

hǣl(u), *health*    men(i)gu, *multitude*
ieldu, *age*    strengu, *strength*,

which were originally of the weak declension (*i*-stems), borrowed the -*u* of the nom. sing. from the ordinary fem. declension, then extended it to other cases, and finally conformed to the ordinary declension.

(*b*) Nouns ending in -ð(*u*) and -*t*(*u*) (earlier -*iðu*), such as

hiehð(u), *height*    ofermēttu, *arrogance*
sǣlð, *happiness*    giemeliest, *neglect*,

belonged from the first to the ordinary declension, but later imitated the uninflected declension of the first class.

NOTES. (1) In (*a*) the sing. is usually indeclinable and plurals are rare.

(2) In (*b*) the ordinary fem. declension is more often followed, and plurals are more common, than in (*a*).

(3) In both classes there has been i-mutation of root-vowels.

(4) For -*u* final, -*o* is frequent.

(5) The uninflected *strengð*, as well as *strengðu*, is found in the accus. sing., but not in EWS.

**30.** *Ēa*, river, and *ǣ*, law, are declined as follows:

*Singular.*

| | | |
|---|---|---|
| N. Acc. | ēa | ǣ, ǣw |
| Gen. | ēa, īe, ēas | ǣ, ǣwe, ǣs |
| Dat. | ēa, īe | ǣ, ǣwe |

*Plural.*

| | | |
|---|---|---|
| N. Acc. | ēa, (ēan *weak*) | ǣ |
| Gen. | ēa | |
| Dat. | ēa(u)m, ēan | |

### (i) *W*-Stems.

**31.** In the following sections attention is called to the special characteristics of *w*-stems, *j*-stems and *i*-stems of all genders, and paradigms are given representing all peculiarities of inflection.

NOTE. The majority of OE. masc. and neuter nouns are *o*-stems, and the majority of fem. nouns *ā*-stems. If the -*o* and -*ā* were preceded by *w* or *j*, the stems are distinguished as *wo*-stems, *wā*-stems and *jo*-stems, *jā*-stems respectively. Next in importance come the *i*-stems, most of which passed over to the *o*- and *ā*- (or "ordinary") declensions.

**32. Paradigms:**

(*a*) Masc.: *bearu*, grove; *ðēo(w)*, servant.
(*b*) Neuter: *bealu*, evil; *trēo(w)*, tree.
(*c*) Fem.: *beadu*, battle; *mǣd*, meadow.

| | Masc. | Neut. | Fem. |
|---|---|---|---|
| | *Singular.* | | |
| Nom. | bearu, -o | bealu, -o | beadu |
| Acc. | ,, | ,, | beadwe |
| Gen. | bearwes | bealwes | ,, |
| Dat. | bearwe | bealwe | ,, |
| | *Plural.* | | |
| N. Acc. | bearwas | bealu, -o | beadwa, -e |
| Gen. | bearwa | bealwa | beadwa |
| Dat. | bearwum | bealwum | beadwum |

## § 32 STRONG NOUNS.

|  | Masc. | Neut. | Fem. |
|---|---|---|---|
|  |  | *Singular.* |  |
| Nom. | ðēo(w) | trēo(w) | mǣd |
| Acc. | ,, | ,, | mǣd(w)e |
| Gen. | ðēowes | trēowes | ,, |
| Dat. | ðēowe | trēowe, trēo | ,, |
|  |  | *Plural.* |  |
| N. Acc. | ðēowas | trēow(u)[1], trēo | mǣd(w)a, -e |
| Gen. | ðēowa | trēowa | mǣd(w)a |
| Dat. | ðēowum | trēowum | mǣd(w)um |

NOTES. (1) It will be seen that these words hardly differ from the ordinary declensions, except in that, when there is no termination, the *w* is vocalised to *u* after a short vowel, and is sometimes dropped after a long vowel. When *w* is retained in the nom., as in *hlǣw*, mound, the ordinary declension is followed throughout.

(2) Decline like bealu    searu, *art*
                  beadu      nearu, *straits*
                             pls. geatwa, getāwa, *equipments*
                                 frætwa, *ornaments*
                 trēo(w)    cnēo(w), *knee*
                 mǣd        læs, *pasture*

(3) The broken vowel in *bearu, bealu*, is carried over from the oblique cases, where *a* is broken regularly before *r, l + w*.

(4) An intrusive vowel is often found before *w*, to ease the pronunciation: exs. *bealowes, bealewa, beaduwe, frætewum* (see § 12).

---

[1] From this final -*u* Cosijn infers that the preceding *eo* in these words was short: see § 9.

## (ii) *J*-**Stems.**

### 33. Paradigms:

(*a*) Masc.: *hęre*, army; *sęcg*, man.
(*b*) Neuter: *rīce*, realm; *fæsten*, stronghold.
(*c*) Fem.: *hālignes*, holiness, sanctuary.

**Masc.**

*Singular.*

| | | |
|---|---|---|
| N. Acc. | hęre | sęcg |
| Gen. | hęr(i)(g)es | sęcges |
| Dat. | hęr(i)(g)e | sęcge |

*Plural.*

| | | |
|---|---|---|
| N. Acc. | hęr(i)(g)(e)as¹ | sęcg(e)as |
| Gen. | hęr(i)g(e)a | sęcg(e)a |
| Dat. | hęr(i)gum | sęcg(i)um |

**Neut.**      **Fem.**

*Singular.*

| | | | |
|---|---|---|---|
| Nom. | rīce | fæsten | hālignes |
| Acc. | ,, | ,, | hālignesse |
| Gen. | rīces | fæsten(n)es | hālignesse |
| Dat. | rīce | fæsten(n)e | hālignesse |

*Plural.*

| | | | |
|---|---|---|---|
| N. Acc. | rīc(i)u | fæsten(n)u | hālignessa, -e |
| Gen. | rīc(e)a | fæsten(n)a | hālignessa |
| Dat. | rīc(i)um | fæsten(n)um | hālignessum |

---

¹ Forms with *g* and without *i* or *e* are common, but never the converse. Thus the forms of the nom. pl. are *hęrigeas, hęrigas, hęrgeas, hęrgas, hęras*.

NOTES. (1) Decline

| *like* **sęcg** | *like* **rīce** |
|---|---|
| hryeg, *back* | stycce, *piece* |
| węcg, *wedge* | gefylce, *troop* |
| lǣce, *leech* | gemierce, *boundary* |
| mēce, *sword* | |

(2) The gemination in the oblique cases of *fæsten* and *hālignes* is found in **all polysyllables** (including disyllables) **ending in -es (-is), -et**, such as *līeget*, lightning; in numerous fem. and neut. derivatives in *-en*, such as *ǣfen* (masc. and neut.), evening, *rǣden* (fem.), arrangement, and all compounds of *-rǣden*; in *condel* (fem.), candle; and in dat. infinitives or gerunds, e.g. *tō beranne, -enne*, to bear.

(3) The above paradigms are grouped together because each of them shows some sign of the original *j* of the stem. (*a*) In *hęre*, *g*, *ig*, *ige* represent earlier *j*; (*b*) in *sęcg*, **the doubled consonant** (cg = gg) after a short vowel represents earlier consonant +*j* (gg < gj), and the mutation of the root-vowel was caused (and in *hęre*) by the *j*; (*c*) in *rīce* and *sęcg*, the palatalisation of the original guttural of the stem, denoted by the intrusive *e*, *i*, is due to the original *j*; (*d*) in *fæsten* and *hālignes*, the doubling of the final consonant in the oblique cases is due to the same cause (see § 13).

(4) *J*-stems presenting no peculiarity of inflection have already been declined in §§ 16, 20, 26.

(5) *Mete*, meat and *hyse*, youth, have passed over in the plural from the *i*-stems to the *j*-stems, as is seen by the doubled consonant: pl. *mettas, metta, mettum; hyssas* (as well as *hysas*).

(iii) *I*-Stems.

### 34. Paradigms:

(*a*) Masc.: *wine*, friend; *Ęngle*, Angles, English.

(*b*) Fem.: *dǣd*, deed.

|           | Masc.            |          | Fem.       |
|-----------|------------------|----------|------------|
|           | *Singular.*      |          |            |
| N. Acc.   | wine             |          | dǣd        |
| Gen.      | wines            |          | dǣde       |
| Dat.      | wine             |          | dǣde       |
|           | *Plural.*        |          |            |
| N. Acc.   | wine, -as        | Engle    | dǣde, -a   |
| Gen.      | wina, wini(g)(e)a| Engla    | dǣda       |
| Dat.      | winum            | Englum   | dǣdum      |

NOTES. (1) The characteristics of this declension are the plurals in *-e*, and the **unchanged acc. sing. of the feminines**. The plural terminations *-as* and *-a* came in from the ordinary declensions. Later came also acc. sing. of feminines in *-e*: *dǣde, cwēne, tīde*, etc.

(2) The neuter *i*-stems do not differ in inflection from the ordinary declension; see *sife* § 20.

(3) Like *Engle* (i.e. without plural in *-as*) are declined a few plurals (without singulars), and names of tribes, nations etc. ending in *-e*:

| Masc. Pls. |        | Nations,    | Tribes          |
|------------|--------|-------------|-----------------|
| lĕode,     | *people* | Mierce,   | *Mercians*      |
| ielde,     | *men*  | Seaxe,      | *Saxons*        |
| ielfe,     | *elves*| Sumorsǣte,  | *men of Somerset* |
|            |        | etc.        |                 |

(4) Like *wine*—the plural in *-as* is much the more frequent— are declined **all mascs. with short mutated vowel + single consonant** + e (except *here*, § 33) such as

| cwide, *speech* | hyge, *mind* | slęge, *stroke* |
| ęge, *terror*   | sige, *victory* | stęde, *place* |

and abstracts in *-scipe*, such as *frēondscipe*, friendship. Only *Dęne*, Dane, has the longer form of the gen. pl.

(5) Like *dǣd* are declined the following feminines, all with long root-syllables and mutated vowels:

| | | |
|---|---|---|
| ǣht, *property* | hȳd, *hide* | tīd, *hour* |
| benc, *bench* | lyft, *atmosphere* | wēn, *expectation* |
| bȳsen, *example* | miht, *might* | wist, *food* |
| cwēn, *woman* | nīed, *need* | wyn(n), *joy* |
| ēst, *favour* | scyld, *guilt* | wyrd, *fate* |
| fierd, *army* | spēd, *success* | wyrt, *root* |

and a few less common words.

(6) The intrusive vowel, to which attention was called in § 33. (1) as marking the palatalisation of the preceding *g* or *c*, is frequently found after those letters in all stems, verbal and adjectival as well as nominal, which originally ended in *i* or *j*. Thus, among *i*-stems, for *men(i)gu* we find *menig(e)o*, and the plural of *wlencu*, pride, is nom. gen. *wlenc(e)a*, dat. *wlenc(i)um*. Of the *i*-stems declined like *wine*, those whose root ends in *g* or *c* sometimes have *e* or *i* before a guttural vowel: *bygeas*, curves, *slegeas*, strokes, etc.; while among long *i*-stems, which have otherwise passed over to the ordinary declension, we find

gleng(e)as, gen. gleng(e)a, *ornaments*   steng(e)as, *poles*
stenc(e)as, *stenches*                    streng(e)as, *strings*
         wrenc(e)as. dat. wrenc(i)um, *wrenches*.

(7) The only *i*-stems which have not a mutated root-vowel are *Seaxe*, *lēode*, *gesceaft*, creation, *geðeaht*, thought, and one or two more. *Seaxe* was originally of the weak declension; hence the gen. pl. *Seaxna*, which has been imitated by *Mierce*, *Miercna*.

(8) *Woruld* (fem.), world, has passed over to the *i*- from the *u*-declension, of which however it sometimes retains the dat. sing. in -a, *worulda*.

**35.** The great majority of OE. nouns belong to the foregoing ordinary declensions. In the following minor and weak declensions, lists or other indications will be given (as has been done already in the case of *w*-stems, *j*-stems and *i*-stems) of the nouns that follow those declensions, so that in what has often been regarded as the difficult problem: "To what declension does a noun belong?" the student has only to **master the lists and criteria given in the various sections** and then to follow this rule: *Ascertain the gender of the noun; apart from any indication to the contrary, it will follow the ordinary declension for that gender.*

W.

## MINOR DECLENSIONS.

### 4. *U*-Stems.

**36. Paradigms:**

(*a*) Short stem: *sunu* (m.), son.
(*b*) Long stem: *hǫnd* (f.), hand.

*Singular.*

|  |  |  |
|---|---|---|
| *N. Acc.* | sunu | hǫnd |
| *Gen.* | suna | hǫnda |
| *Dat.* | suna | hǫnda |

*Plural.*

|  |  |  |
|---|---|---|
| *N. Acc.* | suna | hǫnda |
| *Gen.* | suna | hǫnda |
| *Dat.* | sunum | hǫndum |

NOTES. (1) Several words have passed over to the ordinary declension. Of short stems, *wudu*, wood, *si(o)du*, custom, *duru*, door, *nosu*, nose, are alone fully declined. *Meodu*, mead (drink), has dat. sing. *meodu*, *-o*. *Heoru*, sword, *lagu*, water, *magu*, son, have only nom. acc. sing. All these words are masc. except *duru* and *nosu* (fem.).

Of long stems *hǫnd* alone is fully inflected; but traces of this declension are seen in the dats. sing. *felda* (field), *forda* (ford), *wealda* (forest), *wintra* and *sumera*, and in the occasional gen. sing. *wintra*. All these (except *hǫnd*) are masc. *Winter* has also gen. *wintres*; its plural is neuter, *winter* and *wintru*.

(2) Even the few words given above tend to pass over to the ordinary declension. *Magu* has pl. *magas* even in EWS.; later we find gen. *wudes*, dat. *dure*, *nose*, pl. *sunas*, *wudas*, etc.

(3) The *-u* (*-o*) of the short stems sometimes intrudes into the dat. sing. and nom. acc. pl. For the loss of final *-u* after a long stem see § 9.

## 5. R-Stems.

**37.** Here belong only five names of relatives ending in -r: *fæder*, father, *mōdor*, mother, *brōðor*, brother, *sweostor*, sister, *dohtor*, daughter.

*Singular.*

|  |  |  |  |
|---|---|---|---|
| N. Acc. | fæder | mōdor | brōðor |
| Gen. | fæder, -(e)res | mōdor | brōðor |
| Dat. | fæder | mēder | brēðer |

*Plural.*

|  |  |  |  |
|---|---|---|---|
| N. Acc. | fæd(e)ras | mōdor, mōdru, -a | brōðor, brōðru |
| Gen. | fæd(e)ra | mōdra | brōðra |
| Dat. | fæd(e)rum | mōdrum | brōðrum |

*Singular.*

|  |  |  |
|---|---|---|
| N. Acc. | sweostor | dohtor |
| Gen. | sweostor | dohtor |
| Dat. | sweostor | dehter, dohtor |

*Plural.*

|  |  |  |
|---|---|---|
| N. Acc. | sweostor | dohtor, dohtru, -a |
| Gen. | sweostra | dohtra |
| Dat. | sweostrum | dohtrum |

NOTES. (1) Instead of *-or* we find *-ur*, *-er*, but not *-or* for *-er*. Other forms (mostly later) of *sweostor* are *swostor*, *swuster*, *swyster*. The gens. sing. *mēder* and *dehter* are late. There are collective plurals *gebrōðor*, *-ðru*, brethren, *gesweostor*, sisters.

(2) Hitherto (with the exception of § 25) we have had only strong vowel-stems. The weak *n*-stems are placed last. This and the next two declensions contain irregular consonant-stems. At a later stage these distinctions become fundamental; here simplicity and convenience have been chiefly consulted.

### 6. *ND*-Stems.

**38. Paradigms:** *frēond*, friend; *āgend*, owner.

*Singular.*

| | | |
|---|---|---|
| *N. Acc.* | frēond | āgend |
| *Gen.* | frēondes | āgendes |
| *Dat.* | frīend, frēonde | āgende |

*Plural.*

| | | |
|---|---|---|
| *N. Acc.* | frīend, frēond (*poet.* frēondas) | āgend, -de, -das |
| *Gen.* | frēonda | āgend**ra** |
| *Dat.* | frēondum | āgendum |

NOTE. This class of nouns consists of present participles, which have dropped the final participial -*e* and are used as nouns. Like *frēond* is declined only *fēond*, enemy. **Like *āgend* are declined all polysyllables ending in** -*end*. *Gōddōnd*, (good-doing) benefactor, has pl. *gōddēnd*. Dat. sing. *frēonde* and pl. *āgendas* are borrowed from the ordinary declension. Pl. *āgende* and gen. pl. *āgendra* are borrowed from the declension of adjs. and participles (see § 48). In reading texts, it is often difficult to decide, from the similarity of forms, whether a word is a noun or a participle.

### 7. Other Stems.

**39. Paradigms:**
(*a*) Masc.: *mǫnn*, man; *fōt*, foot.
(*b*) Fem.: *bōc*, book; *hnutu*, nut.

*Singular.*

| | | |
|---|---|---|
| *N. Acc.* | mǫn(n) | fōt |
| *Gen.* | mǫnnes | fōtes |
| *Dat.* | mǫn(n) | fēt |

*Plural.*

| | | |
|---|---|---|
| *N. Acc.* | mǫn(n) | fēt, fōtas |
| *Gen.* | mǫnna | fōta |
| *Dat.* | mǫnnum | fōtum |

## § 39. STRONG NOUNS.

*Singular.*

| | | |
|---|---|---|
| N. Acc. | bōc | hnutu |
| Gen. | bēc, bōce | hnute |
| Dat. | bēc | hnyte |

*Plural.*

| | | |
|---|---|---|
| N. Acc. | bēc | hnyte |
| Gen. | bōca | hnuta |
| Dat. | bōcum | hnutum |

NOTES. (1) The second forms, i.e. those without *i*-mutation, are later.

(2) Like *fōt* is declined *tōð*, tooth.

(3) Like *bōc* are declined

| | | | |
|---|---|---|---|
| brōc, *breeches* | *pl.* brēc | mūs, *mouse* | *pl.* mȳs |
| gōs, *goose* | gēs | turf, *turf* | tyrf |
| lūs, *louse* | lȳs | and a few more. | |

Like *hnutu* is *studu*, column.

(4) The fems. *ni(e)ht*, night, and *mæg(e)ð*, maid, cannot suffer *i*-mutation; they are therefore unchanged in the sing. and the nom. pl. *Ni(e)htes*, by night, is an adverbial formation.

(5) The mascs. *hæleð*, hero, and *mōnað*, month, follow the ordinary declension in the sing., e.g. dat. *mōnðe*; in the pl. they have both *hæleð*, *mōnað* and *hæleðas*, *mōn(e)ðas*.

(6) The declension of the fems. *burg*, walled town, *cū*, cow, and of the neuters *calu*, ale, *scrūd*, dress, is best given in full (as far as the forms are found):

*Singular.*

| | | | | |
|---|---|---|---|---|
| N. Acc. | burg | cū | calu | scrūd |
| Gen. | byr(i)g, burge | cū(e), cȳ, cūs | (e)aloð, -að | |
| Dat. | byr(i)g, burge | cȳ | (e)aloð, -að | scrȳd |

*Plural.*

| | | | | |
|---|---|---|---|---|
| N. Acc. | byr(i)g, burge, -a | cȳ(e) | | scrūd |
| Gen. | burga | cūa, cūna, cȳna | caleða | scrūda |
| Dat. | burgum | cū(u)m | | |

## II. WEAK NOUNS.
### (*n*-stems)

**40. Paradigms:**

(a) Masc.: *guma*, man ; *gefēa*, joy.
(b) Fem.: *heorte*, heart.
(c) Neuter: *ēage*, eye.

|  | Masc. | | Fem. | Neut. |
|---|---|---|---|---|
|  | *Singular.* | | | |
| Nom. | guma | gefēa | heorte | ēage |
| Acc. | guman | gefēan | heortan | ēage |
| Gen. | guman | gefēan | heortan | ēagan |
| Dat. | guman | gefēan | heortan | ēagan |
|  | *Plural.* | | | |
| N. Acc. | guman | gefēan | heortan | ēagan |
| Gen. | gumena | gefēana | heortena | ēag(e)na |
| Dat. | gumum | gefēa(u)m | heortum | ēagum |

NOTES. (1) Like *guma* are declined **all masculines in -a** (except *frēa, wēa* and *rā*).

(2) Like *gefēa* are declined

| *Mascs.* | | | *Fems.* | |
|---|---|---|---|---|
| frēa, *lord* | gen. | frēan | bēo, *bee* | gen. bēon |
| wēa, *woe* | | wēan | tā, *toe* | tān |
| rā, *roe* | | rān | | |
| lēo, *lion* | | lēon | | |
| twēo, *doubt* | | twēon | | |
| pl. Swēon, *Swedes* | | Swēona (dat. Swēom) | | |

(3) Like *heorte* are declined

| ælmesse, *alms* | fæmne, *virgin* | nædre, *adder* |
| cirice, *church* | hearpe, *harp* | sunne, *sun* |
| cwene, *woman* | hlǣfdige, *lady* | tunge, *tongue* |
| corðe, *earth* | miere, *mare* | wice, *week* |

and several others; also a few short-stemmed feminines in -u, such as

    peru, *pear*      ðrotu, *throat*
    spadu, *spade*      wucu, *week*.

(3) Like ēage is declined only ĕare, ear.

(4) The endings -on for -an, and -ona, -ana for -ena, are not uncommon. The e of the gen. pl. may be syncopated in tung(e)na, ĕar(e)na, and in names of peoples after a long root-syllable: Frọnena, Lọngbeardna, etc.

(5) Of common gender are

    cuma, *guest*      gemæcca, *mate*
    gebędda, *bedfellow*      gerẹsta, *spouse*

Eastron, Easter (fem. pl.), is usually indeclinable.

# ADJECTIVES.

**41.** Nearly all OE. adjectives (including participles) have both a Strong (Indefinite) and a Weak (Definite) form: strong *gōd*, weak *gōda*, which follow the strong and the weak declension respectively.

The **weak form** of the adjective is **used**

(*a*) after the definite article and demonstrative adjs.;

(*b*) after a possessive adj.;

(*c*) in the vocative;

(*d*) frequently in poetry where the strong form would be used in prose.

The following adjs. have **only one form.**

(*a*) **Always strong**: ān, one, ōðer, second, āgen, own, hwilc, which, swilc, such, and the possessive adjs. mīn, ðīn, uncer, incer, ūre, ēower.

(*b*) **Always weak:** āna, alone, ilca, same; all ordinals except ōðer; all comparatives; hindema, hindmost. Superlatives have both strong and weak forms; but as they are usually preceded by the definite article, strong forms are not common.

## STRONG DECLENSION.

**42. Endings.**—The strong and weak declensions of adjs. were originally identical with those of strong and weak nouns, but the strong declension has, in several cases, assimilated to the pronominal declension. This will be seen by the following scheme of terminations, in which the distinctively pronominal endings are printed in **black** type, the others in *italic*.

|  | Masc. | Neut. | Fem. |
|---|---|---|---|
|  |  | *Singular.* |  |
| *Nom.* |  |  | (*-u*) |
| *Acc.* | **-ne** |  | *-e* |
| *Gen.* |  | *-es* | **-re** |
| *Dat.* |  | **-um** | **-re** |
| *Instr.* |  | *-e* |  |
|  |  | *Plural.* |  |
| *N. Acc.* | *-e* | (*-u*) | *-a, -e* |
| *Gen.* |  | **-ra** |  |
| *Dat.* |  | *-um* |  |

NOTES. (1) It should be carefully noted: (*a*) that the dat. sing. masc. and neuter, as well as the dat. pl., ends in *-um*; (*b*) that there is an instrumental case in the masc. and neuter sing. distinct from the dat.; (*c*) that a form in *-e* must not be assumed to be a plural; it may be an acc. fem. sing., or an instr. sing.

(2) The rule for the final *-u* of the nom. fem. sing. and neut. pl. is the same as in nouns (see §§ 9, 43).

(3) The following variants are found:
   (*a*) for the *-u* of the nom. fem. sing. occasionally *-o*;
   (*b*) for the *-u* of the neut. pl. sometimes *-o, -a*;
   (*c*) for *-um* (sing. and pl.) occasionally *-on, -an*;
   (*d*) *-ere* for *-re* appears in EWS. in *sum(e)re, hwelcere, ǣlcere*; in late texts *-ere* for *-re* and *-era* for *-ra* become the regular endings.

(e) Long-stemmed (therefore uninflected) neut. pls. sometimes borrow the -e of the masc. pl. even in EWS.: exs. *ealle*, *longe*.

(f) In LWS. the assimilation of terminations becomes more marked: -e tends to become universal in the nom. pl. by replacing the -u of the short-stemmed neuters and ousting the -a of the fems.; and, similarly, the nom. sing. attains one form for all genders by the dropping of the -u of short-stemmed fems.

## 43. Primary paradigms:

(a) Long monosyllable: *gōd*, good.
(b) Short monosyllable: *til*, useful.
(c) Polysyllables: *grēne*, green; *hālig*, holy.

|  | Masc. | Neut. | Fem. |
|---|---|---|---|
|  |  | *Singular.* |  |
| Nom. | gōd | gōd | gōd |
| Acc. | gōdne | gōd | gōde |
| Gen. |  | gōdes | gōdre |
| Dat. |  | gōdum | gōdre |
| Instr. |  | gōde |  |
|  |  | *Plural.* |  |
| N. Acc. | gōde | gōd | gōda, -e |
| Gen. |  | gōdra |  |
| Dat. |  | gōdum |  |
|  |  | *Singular.* |  |
| Nom. | til | til | tilu (§ 9) |
| Acc. | tilne | til | tile |
| Gen. |  | tiles | tilre |
| Dat. |  | tilum | tilre |
| Instr. |  | tile |  |
|  |  | *Plural.* |  |
| N. Acc. | tile | tilu (§ 9) | tila, -e |
| Gen. |  | tilra |  |
| Dat. |  | tilum |  |

|        | Masc.    | Neut.        | Fem.         |
|--------|----------|--------------|--------------|
|        |          | *Singular.*  |              |
| *Nom.* | grēne    | grēne        | grēnu (§ 9)  |
| *Acc.* | grēnne   | grēne        | grēne        |
| *Gen.* |          | grēnes       | grēnre       |
| *Dat.* |          | grēnum       | grēnre       |
| *Instr.* |        | grēne        |              |

|          | *Plural.* | | |
|----------|-----------|---|---|
| *N. Acc.* | grēne | grēnu (§ 9) | grēna, -e |
| *Gen.*    |       | grēnra      |           |
| *Dat.*    |       | grēnum      |           |

|        | Masc.    | Neut.        | Fem.         |
|--------|----------|--------------|--------------|
|        |          | *Singular.*  |              |
| *Nom.* | hālig    | hālig        | hāl(i)gu     |
| *Acc.* | hāligne  | hālig        | hālge        |
| *Gen.* |          | hālges       | hāligre      |
| *Dat.* |          | hālgum       | hāligre      |
| *Instr.* |        | hālge        |              |

|          | *Plural.* | | |
|----------|-----------|---|---|
| *N. Acc.* | hālge | hāl(i)gu | hālga, -e |
| *Gen.*    |       | hāligra  |           |
| *Dat.*    |       | hālgum   |           |

NOTES. (1) Adjs. ending in a double consonant—whether the double consonant be original, as in *eal(l)*, all, *grim(m)*, grim, or < earlier consonant + *j* (*jo*-stems), as in *nyt(t)*, useful—simplify the geminate when final (as a rule) and before a termination beginning with a consonant: exs. gen. masc. *grimmes, nyttes*; acc. masc. *grimne, nytne*. But original *ll* may remain: *eal(l)ne, eal(l)re*.

(2) Like *grēne* are declined **all adjectives ending in -e** (original *j*-stems and *i*-stems).

(3) **Final -u** (see § 9). The almost universal rule for adjs. is, that final -u is retained except in long monosyllables and in disyllables of two short syllables (short + short). Even where in the pl. of neuter nouns it would be dropped, viz. after long + long, it is retained in adjs., e.g. *mēnniscu*. Accordingly we find fem. sing. and neut. pl. *īd(e)lu, āg(e)nu, ōð(e)ru, ēow(e)ru*; but *hefig, micel, monig* (short + short).

Later, however, this distinction was lost and each class borrowed the forms of the other, so that we find on the one hand fem. sing. and neut. pl. *āgen, ēower, hālig, lȳtel*, and on the other *miclu, monegu*.

(4) **Syncope.** The rule laid down in § 10 holds good, i.e. syncope of the *e, i, o*, of the suffixes, *-el, -ol, -er, -or, -ig*, before a termination beginning with a vowel, is normal after a long root-syllable, exceptional after a short. Exceptions are not numerous. *Micel* always syncopates; *yfel* more often than not; adjs. of material in *-en*, such as *gylden*, golden, never (cp. § 22. 2).

(5) It will be seen that the four primary paradigms are practically identical, except as regards final -u and syncope. Rules (3) and (4) just given afford sufficient help for the settlement of these two questions in EWS., and when they are settled, any OE. adj. can be declined by means of the table of endings alone (§ 42).

(6) Slight liberties are sometimes taken with strictly grammatical forms in order to render them easier of pronunciation. Thus if two *n*s come together after another consonant in the acc. masc. sing., the second *n* is apt to be dropped:

| *Nom.* | *Acc. Masc. Sing.* |
|---|---|
| fæcne, *treacherous* | fæcne |
| īsern, *iron* | īsern(n)e |
| sūðerne, *southern* | sūðerne |

Again, a final -*ne*, -*re*, is apt to become -*en*, -*er*, before a termination beginning with a consonant: *frēcne*, dangerous, acc. masc. sing. *frēc(en)ne*; *gifre*, greedy, gen. pl. *gifera*.

(7) Two masc. pl. forms, *monega* and *fēawa* (few), are found with occasional -*a* for -*e*, apparently borrowed from *fela* (indecl.), many.

(8) The pl. adj. *fēawe* (-*a*), *fēa*, few, has dat. *fēawum, fēa(u)m*.

**44. Secondary paradigm:** *glæd*, glad.

|  | Masc. | Neut. | Fem. |
|---|---|---|---|
|  |  | *Singular.* |  |
| *Nom.* | glæd | glæd | gladu |
| *Acc.* | glædne | glæd | glade |
| *Gen.* |  | glades | glædre |
| *Dat.* |  | gladum | glædre |
| *Instr.* |  | glade |  |
|  |  | *Plural.* |  |
| *N. Acc.* | glade | gladu | glada, -e |
| *Gen.* |  | glædra |  |
| *Dat.* |  | gladum |  |

NOTE. In the same way are declined *hwæt*, brisk, *blæc*, black, and all similar adjs. Cp. §§ 17, 21; but observe that here original *a* (§ 100) remains before *every* termination beginning with a vowel.

**45. Secondary paradigm:** *gearu*, ready.

|  | Masc. | Neut. | Fem. |
|---|---|---|---|
|  |  | *Singular.* |  |
| *Nom.* | gearu, -o | gearu, -o | gearu, -o |
| *Acc.* | gearone | gearu, -o | gearwe |
| *Gen.* |  | gearwes | gearore |
| *Dat.* |  | gearwum | gearore |
| *Instr.* |  | gearwe |  |
|  |  | *Plural.* |  |
| *N. Acc.* | gearwe | gearu, -o | gearwa, -e |
| *Gen.* |  | gearora |  |
| *Dat.* |  | gearwum |  |

NOTES. (1) Like *gearu*, a *w(wo)*-stem, are declined *fealu*, fallow, *nearu*, narrow, *geolu*, yellow, and a few less common words. It will be seen that *w* is vocalised to *o* or *u* when final and before a termination beginning with a consonant.

(2) An intrusive *o, u, e*, is frequently found between *r* and *w*: *gearowes, gearuwe, gearewum*. Occasional forms are *gearre, gearra*, for *gearore, gearora*.

### 46. Secondary paradigm: *hēah*, high.

|  | Masc. | Neut. | Fem. |
|---|---|---|---|
|  |  | *Singular.* |  |
| Nom. | hēah | hēah | hēah |
| Acc. | hēan(n)e (hēahne) | hēah | hēa |
| Gen. |  | hēas | hēar(r)e |
| Dat. |  | hēa(u)m, hēagum | hēar(r)e |
| Instr. |  | hēa |  |
|  |  | *Plural.* |  |
| N. A. | hēa | hēa(h) | hēa |
| Gen. |  | hēar(r)a |  |
| Dat. |  | hēa(u)m, hēagum |  |

NOTE. *H*-stems follow the rules laid down in § 13 (q. v.). Thus *hrēoh*, rough, makes *hrēos, hrēone, hrēora, hrēo(u)m*, etc.; *wōh*, crooked, *wōs, wō(u)m*, etc. When the *h* follows a liquid, the preceding vowel is lengthened in compensation for its loss: *ðweorh*, perverse, *ðwēores, ðwēorum*, etc.

## WEAK DECLENSION.

### 47. Paradigm: *gōda*, good.

|  | Masc. | Neut. | Fem. |
|---|---|---|---|
|  |  | *Singular.* |  |
| Nom. | gōda | gōde | gōde |
| Acc. | gōdan | gōde | gōdan |
| Gen. |  | gōdan |  |
| Dat. |  | gōdan |  |
|  |  | *Plural.* |  |
| N. Acc. |  | gōdan |  |
| Gen. |  | gōdra (-ena) |  |
| Dat. |  | gōdum, -an |  |

NOTES. (1) **Variants.** It will be seen that the weak declensions of adjs. and nouns are identical, except in the gen. pl., where weak adjs. usually borrow the strong ending *-ra*. In the dat. pl. *-an* for *-um* is frequent. In all cases ending in *-an*, an occasional *-on* is found.

(2) Syncopated and unsyncopated forms frequently alternate. Syncope is more often admissible than in the strong declension: e.g. adjs. of material in *-en* may syncopate their weak forms, as in dat. pl. *gyldnum*.

(3) *H*-stems contract, etc., much as in the strong declension:

| *Strong.* | *Weak.* |
|---|---|
| hēah, *high* | hēa, hēan, etc. |
| wōh, *crooked* | wō, wōn, wōna, etc. |
| ðweorh, *perverse* | ðwēora, -e, etc. |

## DECLENSION OF PARTICIPLES.

**48. Present participles** terminate in *-ende*, with the exception of those of contracted and some anomalous verbs, which end in *-nde*: *āgende, drincende, giefende, wesende*; *tēonde, slēande, fōnde, bēonde, gānde*. They are declined both strong and weak. The **strong declension** is identical with that of *grēne* (like *grēne*, the pres. part. is a *jo*-stem).

**Paradigm:** *scīnende*, shining.

|  | Masc. | Neut. | Fem. |
|---|---|---|---|
|  |  | *Singular.* |  |
| *Nom.* | scīnende | scīnende | scīnendu |
| *Acc.* | scīnendne | scīnende | scīnende |
| *Gen.* |  | scīnendes | scīnendre |
| *Dat.* |  | scīnendum | scīnendre |
| *Instr.* |  | scīnende |  |
|  |  | *Plural.* |  |
| *N. Acc.* | scīnende | scīnendu | scīnenda, -e |
| *Gen.* |  | scīnendra |  |
| *Dat.* |  | scīnendum |  |

Notes. (1) When used predicatively, uninflected forms are not infrequent, e.g. *scīnende* for *scīnendne*, acc. masc. sing.

(2) The weak declension follows that of *gōda* (§ 47): *scīnenda, -e, -e*.

**49. Past participles** of strong verbs terminate in *-en*, of weak verbs in *-(e)d, -t, -od*. They are declined like ordinary adjectives, both strong and weak.

Final *-u* is irregular. It is more frequent after long roots than after short: neut. pls. *gefongnu, gereafodu; getrymedu*. Past parts. in the predicate (i.e. when not used attributively) rarely take *-u*; indeed fem. and neut. pls. in that position usually take the masc. ending *-e*.

**Syncope** of *e*, in *-en, -ed*, before a vowel, is avoided after short root-syllables. After long root-syllables syncope is optional; but it is frequent in the weak declension, and in past parts. in *-ed*, both strong and weak forms, it is the rule: pls. *gecorene, gebund(e)ne, gefong(e)ne, āworpnan, genęmn(e)de, bedǣlde, oxfæste*. Syncope of the *o* in *-od* does not take place.

## COMPARISON.

### I. Adjectives.

**50.** The comparative of OE. adjs. is formed by adding *-ra* (earlier *-ora*) to the positive, and the superlative by adding *-ost(a)*. Final *-e* is dropped before these endings.

| Pos. | Compar. | Superl. |
|---|---|---|
| heard, *hard* | heardra | heardost(a) |
| hālig, *holy* | hāligra | hāligost(a) |
| nyt(t), *useful* | nyttra | nyttost(a) |
| rīce, *rich* | rīcra | rīcost(a) |
| mǣre, *famous* | mǣrra | mǣrost(a) |
| fæger, *fair* | fægerra | fæg(e)rost(a) |
| gearu, *ready* | gear(o)ra | gearwost(a) |

Adjectives with root-vowel æ retain the original a (see § 100) before the guttural vowel of the superlative ending:

| Pos. | Compar. | Superl. |
|---|---|---|
| glæd, *glad* | glædra | gladost(a) |
| hwæt, *active* | hwætra | hwatost(a) |
| smæl, *small* | smælra | smalost(a) + smælst(a) |

There is a second mode of comparison, in which the prehistoric endings -*ira*, -*ist* (OE. -*ra*, -*est*), caused *i*-mutation of the root-vowel. This mode was followed by a comparatively small number of OE. adjectives:

| | | |
|---|---|---|
| brād, *broad* | brǣdra (brādra) | (brādost(a)) |
| eald, *old* | ieldra | ieldest(a) |
| ēaðe, *easy* | īeðra | īeðest(a) |
| feorr, *far* | fierra | fierrest(a) |
| geong, *young* | giengra | giengest(a) |
| grēat, *great* | grietra | grietest(a) |
| hēah, *high* hīer(r)a | (hīehra, hēahra) | hīehst(a) (hēahst(a)) |
| long, *long* | lengra | lengest(a) |
| nēah, *near* | nēar(r)a | nīehst(a) |
| sceort, *short* | sciertra | sciertest(a) |
| strong, *strong* | strengra | strengest(a) |

NOTES. (1) All comparatives are declined weak; the strong form in -*or* is used for comparative adverbs. Superlatives have both strong and weak forms, -*ost*, -*est*, -*osta*, -*esta*; but the weak form, being used after all demonstratives, is by far the commoner; inflected strong forms are very rare.

(2) Mutated superlatives (above) end in -*est*, the rest in -*ost*; but the former sometimes take -*ost*, and the latter -*est*, especially before a guttural vowel: *fægrestum*. For -*ost* are found -*ast*, -*ust*: *æðelast, wisust*.

(3) The gen. pl. of comparatives usually ends in -*ena*, but there also occur such (strong) gen. pls. as *gearra* for *gearrena*, *ūter(r)a, ūttra*, for *ūterrena*.

### 51. Irregular Comparison.

(*a*) Four adjs. have comparatives and superlatives with a different root from that of the positive:

| Pos. | Compar. | Superl. |
|---|---|---|
| gōd, *good* | bet(e)ra / sēlra, sēlla | bet(e)st / sēlest |
| yfel, *bad, evil* | wiersa | wierrest, wiersta |
| micel, *great* | māra | mǣst |
| lȳtel, *little* | lǣssa | lǣs(es)t |

(*b*) From the adv. ǣr, *before*, are formed the comparative and superlative adjectives ǣr(r)a, ǣrest.

(*c*) **Superlatives in -mest.** The superl. suffix -*ma* is found only in *forma*, first, *hindema*, hindmost; but combined with the further suffix -*est*, it is seen in a number of superlatives, which are etymologically double superlatives. They are mostly without corresponding positive adjs. The comparative usually ends in -*erra*.

| Pos. | Compar. | Superl. |
|---|---|---|
| (norð, *northwards*) | norðerra, nyrðra | norðmest |
| (sūð, *southwards*) | sūðerra, sȳðerra | sūðmest |
| (ēast, *eastwards*) | ēasterra | ēast(e)mest |
| (west, *westwards*) | westerra | west(e)mest |
| mid(d), *middle* | | mid(e)mest |
| (fore, *before*) | | forma, fyrmest, fyr(e)st |
| (forð, *forth*) | furðra | |
| (æfter, *after*) | æft(er)ra | æftemest |
| (ufan, *above*) | yferra, uferra | yfemest, ufemest (ymest) |
| niðan, *below*) | niðerra | niðemest |
| inne, *within*) | innerra | innemest |
| ūte, *without*) | yterra, ūterra | yt(e)mest, ūtemest |
| læt, *late* | lætra | lætemest, lætest |
| sīð, *late*, adv.) | sīðra | sīð(e)mest, sīðest |

## II. Adverbs.

**52.** As a rule, only adverbs formed from adjectives can be compared. The comparative is formed by adding *-or*, the superlative by adding *-ost*, to the positive adv., after cutting off final *-e*. Thus the strong forms of comparative and superlative adjs. are used as compar. and superl. advs.

| Pos. | Compar. | Superl. |
|---|---|---|
| hearde, *hard* | heardor | heardost |
| dēope, *deeply* | dēopor | dēopost |
| fæste, *fast* | fæstor | fæstost |
| gear(w)e, *well* | gear(w)or | gear(w)ost |

The comparative in *-or* is never used as an adjective.

**53. Irregular Comparison.**

(*a*) It will have been noticed that the place of the positive of most of the words compared in § 51 was supplied by an adverb. Several of these advs. have compars. in *-or*—norðor, sūðor, furðor, ufor, niðor, innor, ūtor—and the superl. adjs. are equally used as advs.

(*b*) The following have monosyllabic comparatives, almost all with mutated root-vowels:

| | | |
|---|---|---|
| wel, *well* | { bet | bet(o)st |
| | sēl | sēlest |
| yfle, *ill* | wiers | wierrest |
| lȳt(el), *little* | lǣs | lǣst |
| micle, *much* | mā, mǣ | mǣst |
| feorr, *far* | fierr | fierrest |
| nēah, *nigh* | nēar, nȳr | nīehst |
| ǣr, *before* | ǣr, ǣror | ǣrost, ǣr(e)st |
| sīð, *late* | sīð, sīðor | sīð(e)mest, sīðest |
| lǫnge, *long* | lęng | lęngest |
| ēaðe, *easily* | īeð | ēaðost |
| sōfte, *softly* | sēft | sōftest |

# NUMERALS.

**54.** The OE. numerals are as follows:

| | Cardinal | Ordinal |
|---|---|---|
| 1 | ān | forma, ǣrest(a), fyrmest(a), fyr(e)st(a) |
| 2 | twēgen, **twā, tū** | ōðer, æfterra |
| 3 | ðrīe, ðrēo | ðridda |
| 4 | fēower | fēorða |
| 5 | fīf | fīfta |
| 6 | siex | siexta |
| 7 | seofon | seofoða |
| 8 | eahta | eahtoða |
| 9 | nigon | nigoða |
| 10 | tīen | tēoða |
| 11 | ęn(d)lefan | ęn(d)lefta |
| 12 | twęlf | twęlfta |
| 13 | ðrītīene, ðrēotīene | ðrēotēoða |
| 14 | fēowertīene | fēowertēoða |
| 15 | fīftīene | fīftēoða |
| 16 | siextīene | siextēoða |
| 17 | seofontīene | seofontēoða |
| 18 | eahtatīene | eahtatēoða |
| 19 | nigontīene | nigontēoða |
| 20 | twēntig | twēntigoða |
| 21 | ān ǫnd **twēntig** | ān ǫnd twēntigoða |
| 30 | ðrītig | ðrītigoða |
| 40 | fēowertig | fēowertigoða |
| 50 | fīftig | fīftigoða |
| 60 | siextig | siextigoða |
| 70 | hundseofontig | hundseofontigoða |
| 80 | hundeahtatig | hundeahtatigoða |
| 90 | hundnigontig | hundnigontigoða |
| 100 | hundtēontig, **hund, hundred** | hundtēontigoða |

| | | |
|---|---|---|
| 101 | ān hund ond ān | ān ond hundtēontigoða |
| 110 | hundendlefantig | hundendlefantigoða |
| 120 | hundtwelftig | hundtwelftigoða |
| 200 | tū (twā) hund | |
| 300 | ðrēo hund | |
| 1000 | (ān) ðūsend | |

NOTES. (1) The ordinals follow the weak declension, with the exception of ōðer, which is always strong, and ǣrest(a), fyrmest(a), fyrest(a), which are both strong and weak (like other superlatives).

(2) OE. has numerals like German anderthalb (second half), one and a half, vierthalb (fourth half), three and a half, etc. Thus we find feorðe healf hund scipa, 350 ships; fīfte healf hund = 450; ōðer healf hund = 150.

(3) Slight variations in the endings are met with, such as -eða for oða in eahteða, eighth; -tiogoða, -teogða, -tēoða for -tigoða.

(4) The formation of the numerals 70, 80, 90, 100, 110, 120, has not been satisfactorily explained.

(5) There are no ordinals for 200 and upwards.

## 55. Declension of Cardinals.

(a) **Ān**, one, is declined as follows:

| | Masc. | Neut. | Fem. |
|---|---|---|---|
| Nom. | ān | ān | ān |
| Acc. | ānne, ǣnne | ān | āne |
| Gen. | ānes | | ānre |
| Dat. | ānum | | ānre |
| Instr. | āne, ǣne | | |

NOTES. (1) Plural forms (like those of gōd, § 43) are rare, but the gen. pl. occurs in the phrase ānra gehwile, each one.

(2) The weak form āna means "alone."

(b) **Twēgen**, two.

| | | | |
|---|---|---|---|
| N. Acc. | twēgen | tū, twā | twā |
| Gen. | | twēg(e)a, twēgra | |
| Dat. | | twǣm, twām | |

§ 55   NUMERALS.   53

With this cp. the declension of *bēgen*, both:

|  | Masc. | Neut. | Fem. |
|---|---|---|---|
| N. Acc. | bēgen | bū | bā |
| Gen. |  | bēg(r)a |  |
| Dat. |  | bǣm, bām |  |

NOTE. (3) Here there is some tendency to confusion of genders. The fem. form *twā* is used for the neuter. *Bā* and *twā* are often conjoined, and then *bā twā* is masc. and fem., and *bū tū* (also in one word) neuter.

(c) **Ðrie**, three.

|  | | | |
|---|---|---|---|
| N. Acc. | ðrīe | ðrēo | ðrēo |
| Gen. |  | ðrēora |  |
| Dat. |  | ðrim |  |

(d) **4 to 19** are indeclinable when used as adjs. (i.e. with a noun); they are declined like *Engle* (§ 34). *-a*, *-um*, when used absolutely. Exs.:

feowera sum, *one of four*, i.e. with three others;

ðāra twelf hēahfæderа, *of the twelve patriarchs*.

(e) **20 to 120** (multiples of ten only) were originally neuter nouns governing a gen., but are also used as adjs. They are sometimes uninflected, sometimes have a gen. in *-es*, but most commonly have gen. in *-ra*, *-a*, dat. in *-um*. Exs.:

hundseofontig mīla, 70 *miles*;

eahta ond feowertiges elna long, 48 *ells long*;

æfter ðrītigra daga fæce, *after the space of 30 days*;

æfter siextegum daga, *after 60 days*;

ðrītigum nihtum ǣr, 30 *days before*.

(f) **Hund**, hundred, is usually uninflected, but in EWS. has a dat. (= dat. pl.) in *-e*; in either case it usually governs a gen.:

fiftīene hund ðūsend monna, 1,500,000 *men*;

mid feower hunde scipa, *with 400 ships*.

(g) **Dūsend**, thousand, has the inflections of a neuter noun, gen. ðūsendes, pl. ðūsend, -u, -o, gen. -a (-ra), dat. -um ; it is also uninflected:

fela ðūsenda (gen. pl.) ofslægenra, *many thousands of slain*;
ðūsend monna bigleofa, *the food of a thousand men*.

(h) In **compound numbers**, both cardinal and ordinal, the smaller numerals remain uninflected:

ðāra twā ond twēntigra monna, *of those twenty-two men*;
fēower hunde wintrum & fēower & siextigum (dat.), *464 years*;
on ðǣm ān ond ðrītigoðan psalme, *in the 31st psalm*;

but exceptionally (possibly by attraction):

on ðǣm twǣm ond on fēowerteogðan gēare, *in the 42nd year*.


# PRONOUNS AND ADJECTIVE-PRONOUNS.

## I. PERSONAL[1].

**56.** First Person, *ic*, I ; Second Person, ðū, thou.

|  | Sing. | Dual. | Plural. |
|---|---|---|---|
| *Nom.* | ic | wit | wē |
| *Acc.* | mec, mē | uncit, unc | ūsic, ūs |
| *Gen.* | mīn | uncer | ūser, ūre |
| *Dat.* | mē | unc | ūs |
| *Nom.* | ðū | git | gē |
| *Acc.* | ðec, ðē | incit, inc | ēowic, ēow |
| *Gen.* | ðīn | incer | ēower |
| *Dat.* | ðē | inc | ēow |

NOTE. (1) The accusatives *mec, ðec, uncit, incit, ūsic, ēowic*, are early or poetical.

---

[1] *Hē, hēo, hit*, is properly a demonstrative pronoun of the 3rd person, being used to indicate *things and persons alike*.

Third Person, *hē* (m.), he, it ; *hēo* (f.), she, it ; *hit* (n.), it.

|  | Masc. | Neut. | Fem. |
|---|---|---|---|
|  |  | *Singular.* |  |
| *Nom.* | hē | hit | hēo (hīe) |
| *Acc.* | hine | hit | hīe (hēo) |
| *Gen.* |  | his | hiere |
| *Dat.* |  | him | hiere |
|  |  | *Plural.* |  |
| *N. Acc.* |  | hīe (hēo), *they* |  |
| *Gen.* |  | hiera, heora |  |
| *Dat.* |  | him |  |

NOTE. (2) There are numerous alternative forms with which the above and the following declensions might be cumbered and obscured. Generally it may be said, that *i* may be found for *ie*, and *io*, *īo* for *eo*, *ēo*, and *io* for *i* followed in the next syllable by a guttural vowel ; later **i, y, for ie (short and long) is universal,** and *i* and *y* interchange pretty freely. See Part II. Special LWS. forms are nom. pl. *hig*, dat. pl. *heom* (to distinguish from the sing.).

## II. REFLEXIVE.

**57.** The possessive *sīn*, his, her, its, is the only relic of a reflexive pronoun in OE. The personal pronouns of all persons are used reflexively, both with and without *self*, which is declined like a strong adj.: *ic self, ðū selfne, him selfum, ūre selfra, ēow selfum,* etc. Sometimes *self* appears to be uninflected, when it really agrees with the subject, not with the pron. with which it is conjoined : *God foresceawað him self ðā offrunge,* God [him]self will provide for him[self] the offering. The weak form *selfa* is also found : *God selfa ;* but, except in the nom. sing. masc., it usually occurs after the def. art. in the sense of *se ilca,* the same.

## III. POSSESSIVE (Adjectives).

**58.** The genitive cases of the personal prons. are used as possessive adjs.: **mīn, ðīn, uncer, incer, ūre (ūser), ēower**, *are fully inflected* according to the strong declension; **his, hiere, hiera**, *are indeclinable*, and may therefore be parsed, at will, as indeclinable poss. adjs., or as personal prons. in the gen. case.

**Paradigm**: ūre, *our*.

|  | Masc. | Neut. | Fem. |
|---|---|---|---|
|  |  | *Singular.* |  |
| *Nom.* | ūre | ūre | ūre (*not* ūru) |
| *Acc.* | ūrne | ūre | ūre |
| *Gen.* | ūres |  | ūr(r)e |
| *Dat.* | ūrum |  | ūr(r)e |
| *Instr.* | ūre |  |  |
|  |  | *Plural.* |  |
| *N. Acc.* |  | ūre |  |
| *Gen.* |  | ūr(r)a |  |
| *Dat.* |  | ūrum |  |

NOTES. (1) *Ēower*, your, syncopates the *e* before a vowel, and may even contract *ēowerre, ēowerra,* to *ēowre, ēowra*. Its nom. pl. neut. is *ēowru*.

(2) *Ūser* = *ūre*, our, assimilates *sr* to *ss* in the syncopated forms: dat. *ūssum* = *ūrum*.

(3) *Sīn*, his, her, its, is poetic.

(4) *Ūre* and *ēower*, when they are gen. pls. of the personal pronouns and not possessive adjectives, are apt to be attracted into agreement with the following word, on which in reality they depend: *ēowra selfra onweald* = *ēower selfra onweald*, rule over yourselves; *ūres nānes* = *ūre nānes*, of none of us.

## IV. DEMONSTRATIVE.

**59.** (a) **Sē, sēo, ðæt,** the, that.

|  | Masc. | Neut. | Fem. |
|---|---|---|---|
|  |  | *Singular.* |  |
| *Nom.* | sē | ðæt | sēo |
| *Acc.* | ðone | ðæt | ðā |
| *Gen.* |  | ðæs | ðǣre |
| *Dat.* |  | ðǣm (ðām) | ðǣre |
| *Instr.* |  | ðȳ (ðon) |  |
|  |  | *Plural.* |  |
| *N. Acc.* |  | ðā |  |
| *Gen.* |  | ðāra (ðǣra) |  |
| *Dat.* |  | ðǣm (ðām) |  |

NOTE. The instrumental ðon is almost always neuter, being used chiefly either with adverbial force, as in ðon mā, the more, or in adverbial phrases, for ðon, on that account, to ðon, to that extent, etc., or in compound conjunctions, ǣr ðon ðe, before, etc. The other forms in parentheses are later.

(b) **Ðes, ðēos, ðis,** this.

|  | Masc. | Neut. | Fem. |
|---|---|---|---|
|  |  | *Singular.* |  |
| *Nom.* | ðes | ðis | ðēos |
| *Acc.* | ðisne | ðis | ðās |
| *Gen.* |  | ðis(s)es | ðisse |
| *Dat.* |  | ðis(s)um | ðisse |
| *Instr.* |  | ðȳs |  |
|  |  | *Plural.* |  |
| *N. Acc.* |  | ðās |  |
| *Gen.* |  | ðissa |  |
| *Dat.* |  | ðis(s)um |  |

NOTE. This adj.-pron. is compounded of the demonstrative sē (North. ðe) and the particle -se = behold.

## V. RELATIVE.

**60.** The place of a relative pronoun, which OE. lacks, is supplied in four ways:

(*a*) By the demonstrative *sē, sēo, ðæt*, used as a relative of the **3rd person**. Ex.: ān æstel, sē bið on fīftegum mancessa, *a bookmark, which shall be worth fifty half-crowns.*

(*b*) By *sē, sēo, ðæt*, immediately followed by the particle ðe: sē ðe, sēo ðe, ðæt ðe (ðætte)—**3rd person** only. Ex.: suma bēc, ðā ðe nīedbeðearfosta sīen, *some books, which may be most necessary.*

NOTE. (1) If *sē* etc., is separated from ðe, it is to be regarded as the antecedent, not as part of the relative; we also find *sē* (antec.)...*sē* ðe (rel.).

(*c*) By the particle ðe alone—**all persons**. Ex.: wīsdōm ðe ðē God sealde, *wisdom which God gave thee.*

(*d*) By the particle ðe followed by a personal pronoun of **any person**: ðe ic, (I) who; ðe ðū (thou) who; ðe hine, whom. Ex.: nis nū cwicra nān, **ðe ic him** mōdsefan mīnne durre āsecgan, *there is now no one of the living to whom I dare unburden my heart.*

NOTE. (2) Other words, as in the above ex., may intervene between ðe and the following personal pronoun, especially in the genitive of the 3rd person: ðe...his, ðe...hiere, ðe...hiera, whose.

## VI. INTERROGATIVE.

**61. Hwā, hwæt,** who? what?

|  | Masc. |  | Neut. |
|---|---|---|---|
| *Nom.* | hwā |  | hwæt |
| *Acc.* | hwone |  | hwæt |
| *Gen.* |  | hwæs |  |
| *Dat.* |  | hwǣm, hwām |  |
| *Instr.* |  | hwȳ (hwon) |  |

NOTES. (1) *Hwā, hwæt*, like *hwæðer* (which of two) and *hwilc* (which), is an interrogative (both direct and indirect) and indefinite pronoun, but not a relative pronoun.

(2) The instrumental *hwon* (cp. ðon) is only used in adverbial phrases, such as *for hwon, tō hwon,* why.

## VII. INDEFINITE.

**62. Hwā, hwæt**, someone, something, **hwæðer**, one of two, and hwilc (hwelc, hwylc), any(one), are used as indefinite pronouns in interrogative and negative sentences. They may all three be compounded with ā-, ge-, and ā + ge (< gi) > ǣg-, so that we get the following scheme of indefinite pronouns:

|       | hwā :            | hwæðer :                  | hwilc :              |
|-------|------------------|---------------------------|----------------------|
| ā-    | āhwā, *anyone*   | āhwæðer, *one of two*     | āhwilc, *whatsoever* |
| ge-   | gehwā, *each one*| gehwæðer, *both*          | gehwilc, *each*      |
| ǣg-   | ǣghwā, *each one*| ǣghwæðer, *either, each*  | ǣghwilc, *each.*     |

These, together with

āwiht, *aught, anything*      swelc, *such*
ǣlc, *each*      swā hwā swā, *whoever*
ǣnig, *any*      swā hwilc swā, *whichever*,

are the most important indef. prons. in OE.

NOTES. (1) The declension of hwā is given in § 61. All the other words mentioned above (except āwiht, -es, -e) are declined like strong adjs.

(2) Hwā and its compounds and āwiht are substantive pronouns; the others are adj.-prons., i.e. may be used either as prons. or in agreement with a noun.

(3) To several of the above words n can be prefixed, and thus the corresponding negative word is obtained: nǣnig, nān, none, nāwiht, naught, nāhwæðer, neither.

(4) Some of the above words have forms and contractions that differ from one another very considerably. Thus ǣghwæðer > ǣgðer = either; āhwæðer = ōhwæðer > ō(w)ðer; nāwiht = nāwuht > nā(u)ht = naught, and so on.

## VERBS.

**63.** OE. verbs are divided into two main classes, Strong and Weak, and two minor classes, Past-Present and Anomalous. They have four moods, infinitive, indicative, subjunctive, and imperative (present); only two tenses, present and past (the pres. is often used as a future); two numbers and three persons; two participles, present (active) and past (passive). The infinitive has a dative case governed by *tō* which is often called the gerund. The passive voice is simply made up of the verb *wesan*, *bēon*, to be, followed by a past part., and is therefore not treated of here[1].

The **principal parts** of a verb are the infinitive, past singular, past plural, and past participle. To these is often added the 3rd sing. pres. indic. In weak verbs the past pl. is omitted, because in them it is formed from the past sing. (See §§ 67, 83.)

**64. Strong Verbs and Weak Verbs.**—Strong verbs may be distinguished from weak verbs in several ways:

(*a*) **By the formation of the past tense.** Strong verbs form their past tense by gradation of the root-vowel, as in *wrītan*, *wrāt*, write, wrote; weak verbs by adding the termination -*de* (-*te*) to the root. This is the main distinction. There is no gradation in weak verbs; there are no past tenses in -*de*, -*te*, in strong verbs.

(*b*) The past part. of strong verbs ends in -*en*, of weak verbs in -*d*, -*t*.

NOTE. The past part. also is formed by gradation in strong verbs. But, since Classes V, VI and VII have the same vowel in the past part. as in the infin., this is a much less conclusive test of a strong past part. than the ending.

(*c*) The roots of strong verbs are monosyllabic. All polysyllabic roots belong to the weak conjugation.

---

[1] The only relic of pass. inflection is in the forms *hātte* (sing.), *hātton* (pl.). pres. and past of *hātan*, to be called.

(d) Strong verbs are original; a word showing the same root as a strong verb is derived from one of its stems. Weak verbs are derivative.

(e) Many strong verbs are intransitive; most transitive verbs are weak, and many have been formed from strong intrans. verbs:

| Strong. | | Weak. |
|---|---|---|
| cp. cwelan, die | and | cwellan, kill; |
| licgan, lie | ,, | lęcgan, lay; |
| sittan, sit | ,, | sęttan, set; |
| beornan, burn (intrans.) | ,, | bærnan, burn (trans.). |

(f) Weak verbs originally joined all present endings to the root by means of j or i, and this j or i has remained in the infins. in -ian (nęrian, lufian), and has left traces in the mutation of root-vowels (hīeran) and in the doubled consonants (< consonant + j) after a short root-vowel (fręmman). Nearly all weak verbs in -an and a few in -ian have mutated root-vowels. **No strong verbs** (except those with *weak* presents) **have** infins. in -ian, **or mutated root-vowels, or doubled**[1] **consonants.**

NB. A *mutated* root-vowel (§ 3) *therefore infallibly denotes a weak verb* (or a "weak present," § 80).

(g) On the other hand, a mutated vowel in the 2nd and 3rd sing. pres., with an unmutated root-vowel in the infin., is a mark of strong verbs (§ 68); weak verbs have the same vowel, whether mutated or unmutated, in the infin. and in the 2nd and 3rd sing. pres.

(h) The following are characteristic of weak verbs (but not of all weak verbs): i, ig, ige before the endings -an, -anne, -að, -e, -en, -ende; 2nd and 3rd sing. pres. in -ast, -að; imperative sing. in -e or -a.

NB. Tests (f), (g), (h) are useless for a dozen strong verbs with *weak presents*, for which see § 80.

---

[1] *Doubled*, not *double*. The strong verbs *feallan, weallan, bonnan,* etc., have original *double* consonants, not *doubled* before j.

**65. Endings.**—For the sake of comparison a scheme of the normal endings of strong and weak verbs respectively is here given, but they will be better learnt in the paradigms of the verbs themselves.

|  | Strong. | Weak. | |
|---|---|---|---|
|  |  | Classes I., II. | III. |

*Present Indicative.*

| | | | |
|---|---|---|---|
| Sing. 1. | -e | -e | -ie |
| 2. | -(e)st | -(e)st | -ast |
| 3. | -(e)ð | -(e)ð | -að |
| Plur. 1, 2, 3. | -að | -að | -iað |

*Present Subjunctive.*

| | | | |
|---|---|---|---|
| Sing. 1, 2, 3. | -e | -e | -ie |
| Plur. 1, 2, 3. | -en | -en | -ien |

*Past Indicative.*

| | | | |
|---|---|---|---|
| Sing. 1. |  | -(e)de, -te | -ode |
| 2. | -e | -(e)dest, -test | -odest |
| 3. |  | -(e)de, -te | -ode |
| Plur. 1, 2, 3. | -on | -(e)don, -ton | -odon |

*Past Subjunctive.*

| | | | |
|---|---|---|---|
| Sing. | -e | -(e)de, -te | -ode |
| Plur. | -en | -(e)den, -ten | -oden |

*Imperative.*

| | | | |
|---|---|---|---|
| Sing. 2. |  | (-e) | -a |
| Plur. 2. | -að | -að | -iað |

*Infinitive.*

| | | | |
|---|---|---|---|
|  | -an | -an | -ian |

*Participles.*

| | | | |
|---|---|---|---|
| Pres. | -ende | -ende | -iende |
| Past. | -en | -(e)d, -t | -od |

NOTE. It must be remembered that, as will be seen from the following paradigm, the gradation of the root-vowel in strong verbs is more important than the endings for distinguishing one part of the verb from another and for distinguishing a strong from a weak verb.

## 1. STRONG VERBS.

**66. Paradigm:** *rīdan*, ride.

### Indicative.

|  | | Present. | Past. |
|---|---|---|---|
| *Sing.* | 1. | rīde | rād |
|  | 2. | rīdest, rītst | ride |
|  | 3. | rīdeð, rīt(t) | rād |
| *Plur.* | | rīdað | ridon |

### Subjunctive.

| | Present. | Past. |
|---|---|---|
| *Sing.* | rīde | ride |
| *Plur.* | rīden | riden |

### Imperative.

| | |
|---|---|
| *Sing.* | rīd |
| *Plur.* | rīdað |

### Infinitive.

rīdan, *dat.* -anne.

### Participles.

rīdende          geriden

**Variants.** (*a*) Instead of the pres. subj. plur. *rīden* we regularly find *rīde*, when the prons. *wē, gē*, follow immediately: *rīde wē, gē* (a kind of jussive subjunctive), let us ride, ride (ye). This usage was extended to the pres. and past indic., so that *rīde gē ?* = do ye ride? and *ride gē ?* = did ye ride?

This remark applies equally to weak verbs; as also do the following as far as weak verbs have the same terminations.

(*b*) Past parts. of both strong and weak verbs usually have the prefix *ge-*, which is, however, rarely found before another prefix.

(c) The original endings of the sing. pres. indic. were: 1st pers. -u, -o; 2nd pers. -is > -es; 3rd pers. -ið. Hence the *i*-mutation of the root-vowel (there can be no *i*-mutation of *i*) in the 2nd and 3rd sing. pres. indic. of strong verbs (§ 68).

(d) The final -t of the 2nd pers. sing. is the emaciated remnant of ðū, thou; a few forms ending in -sð are extant: *rides* + ðū > *ridesð* > *ridest*. Similarly, an epithetic -t has been added to the 2nd sing. past of weak verbs.

(e) The past indic. pl. originally ended in -*un*; later texts often have -*an*.

(f) The subjunctive pl. *pres.* frequently ends in -*an*; in the *past*, later texts often take over the -*on* of the indic.

(g) The usual ending of the dative iufin. or gerund is -*anne*, but -*en(n)e* (§ 33) is not uncommon.

**67. Principal Parts.**—It will be seen from the paradigm given in § 66 that, through the *gradation* of the root-vowel, the strong verb *rīdan* has at least three different stems: *rīd-*, *rād-*, *rid-*. The number of different stems in a strong verb is sometimes four, as in *bēod*-an, *bēad*, *bud*-on, *bod*-en; *ber*-an, *bær*, *bǣr*-on, *bor*-en. We say then that the OE. strong verb has **four stems**, which are *not necessarily different*. These four stems are best shown in the four principal parts: (1) infin., (2) past sing., (3) past pl., (4) past part., as seen in the examples just given. Thus the importance of knowing the principal parts of a strong verb is evident, because all the other parts are formed from them *by simply changing the endings as shown in the paradigm of* § 66. The following scheme shows **what parts are formed from each of the principal parts**:

| From | Are formed | Tenses. |
|---|---|---|
| **Infinitive** | *All present forms* | Pres. Indic.<br>Pres. Subj.<br>Imperative.<br>Pres. Part. |
| **Past 1st and 3rd Sing.**<br>**Past Plur.** | *None*<br>*All past forms* | Past Indic.<br>2nd Sing.<br>Past Subj. |
| **Past Part.** | **Passive Voice** only. | |

## 2nd and 3rd Singular Present.

**68.** It will have been noticed that two forms, syncopated and unsyncopated, of the 2nd and 3rd sing. pres. indic. were given in the paradigm of *ridan*. Moreover, a verb with root-vowel *i* was purposely chosen because there would have been mutation of almost any other vowel in the above parts (as explained in § 66 c). These two things then demand a little attention in forming the 2nd and 3rd sing. pres. of strong verbs: (i) Mutation of root-vowel; (ii) Syncope, and consequent changes.

(i) **Mutation of root-vowel.** *Rule:* Form the 2nd and 3rd sing. pres. indic. of strong verbs with mutated root-vowel, according to the following scheme:

| Original Vowel | Mutated Vowel | Infin. | 3rd Sing. |
|---|---|---|---|
| a | æ (§ 121) | faran, *go* | færð |
| ā | ǣ | blāwan, *blow* | blǣwð |
| e | i (§§ 98, 120) | helpan, *help* | hilpð |
| ea | ie | healdan, *hold* | hielt |
| ēa | īe | hēawan, *hew* | hīewð |
| eo | ie (§ 120) | weorðan, *become* | wierð |
| ēo | īe (§ 120) | crēopan, *creep* | criepð |
| o | e | stondan, *stand* | stent |
| ō | ē | blōwan, *bloom* | blēwð |
| u | y | cuman, *come* | cymð |
| ū | ȳ | brūcan, *enjoy* | brȳcð |
| e, i, ī, ie, ǣ | | are not affected by *i*-mutation. | |

NOTES. (1) Empirical rules for forming the 2nd and 3rd sing. pres. from the infin. are often helpful and usually harmless. But it must be clearly understood that these parts are not *derived* from the OE. infin., but from their own earlier prehistoric forms, and it is at times of the utmost importance that the fact

W. 5

should be as clearly stated. Thus *bireð* can be traced step by step from the Indo-Germanic form *bhereti*; to say that it is formed from the root of *beran* by the addition of -*eð*, with mutation of the root-vowel, is certainly both inaccurate and misleading.

(2) Syncopated forms with mutated vowels, as above, are the rule in EWS., although unsyncopated forms both with mutated and with unmutated vowels are also found: *bireð* from *beran*, *bȳgeð* from *būgan*, *weorðeð* from *weorðan*.

(3) Unsyncopated forms without *i*-mutation are the rule in Anglian.

**69.** (ii) **Syncope, etc.** The *e* of the endings -*est*, -*eð*, in the 2nd and 3rd sing. pres. indic., is regularly dropped in EWS., and the following changes take place in the consonants thus brought together.

NB. *These changes are not peculiar to strong verbs, but take place also in weak verbs (Classes 1 and 2) when the specified conditions are present.*

Persons.

**2nd, 3rd.** (a) Double consonants are simplified: *winn(e)st* > *winst*, *winn(e)ð* > *winð*; *fyll(e)st* > *fylst*, *fyll(e)ð* > *fylð*.

**2nd.** (b) Before -*st*, *d* > *t*, and *s*, *ð* and *st* are dropped: *find(e)st* > *fintst*; *stend(e)st* > *stentst*; *cīes(e)st* > *cīest*; *wierð(e)st* > *wierst*; *cwið(e)st* > *cwist*; *birst(e)st* > *birst*.

**3rd.** (c) *d* or *t* + *ð* > *t* after a consonant, > *tt* or *t* after a vowel: *find(e)ð* > *fint*; *birst(e)ð* > *birst* (thus the 2nd and 3rd sing. of stems ending in *st* became identical); *fæst(e)ð* > *fæst*; *būd(e)ð* > *būt(t)*; *grēt(e)ð* > *grēt(t)*; *set(e)ð* > *sett*. Similarly *ð* + *ð* > *ð* after a consonant, > *ðð* or *ð* after a vowel: *wierð(e)ð* > *wierð*; *cwið(e)ð* > *cwið(ð)*.

**3rd.** (d) *s* + *ð* usually > -*st*, but in early texts -*sð* also remains: *forlīes(e)ð* > *forlīest*; *wiex(e)ð* > *wiext* (x = h + s); *cīes(e)ð* > *cīest* (thus the 2nd and 3rd sing. of stems ending in *s* became identical).

**2nd, 3rd.** (e) *g* sometimes > *h* before -*st* and -*ð*, but chiefly in later texts: *stig(e)st* > *stihst*; *lieg(e)ð* > *liehð*.

NB. The above rules are given here in order that the succeeding sections on "gradation," with which they have properly nothing to do, may not be cumbered with them, and because they could not be postponed till later. The student must pay due attention to them, so that, when gradation has been mastered, he may be in a position to conjugate in full every OE. strong verb. One or two examples from each strong class are appended ("weak presents" and contracted verbs are treated separately); the 2nd and 3rd sing. pres. of every verb mentioned in the following §§ should be written out in the same way.

| Class | Infin. | 2nd Sing. | 3rd Sing. |
|---|---|---|---|
| I. ("Shine") | ārīsan, *arise* | ārīst | ārīst |
| | bīdan, *wait* | bītst | bīt(t) |
| | bītan, *bite* | bītst | bīt(t) |
| | mīðan, *avoid* | mīst | mīð(ð) |
| II. ("Creep") | bēodan, *order* | bīetst | bīet(t) |
| | scēotan, *shoot* | scīetst | scīet(t) |
| | lūcan, *lock* | lȳcst | lȳcð |
| IIIa. ("Help") | helpan, *help* | hilpst | hilpð |
| | feohtan, *fight* | fiehtst | fieht |
| b. ("Drink") | drincan, *drink* | drincst | drincð |
| IV. ("Bear") | beran, *bear* | bir(e)st | bir(e)ð |
| V. ("Tread") | tredan, *tread* | tritst | trit(t) |
| VI. ("Fare") | faran, *go* | færst | færð |
| VII. (Reduplicating) | blāwan, *blow* | blǣwst | blǣwð |
| | lǣtan, *let* | lǣtst | lǣt(t) |
| | healdan, *hold* | hieltst | hielt |
| | hēawan, *hew* | hīewst | hīewð |
| | blǫndan, *blend* | blęntst | blęnt |
| | blōwan, *bloom* | blēwst | blēwð |

# GRADATION (*Ablaut*).

**70.** Strong verbs are conjugated principally by the use of different stems in the same verb, these stems being related to one another by the "gradation" of the root-vowel without other change. **Gradation** in OE. then may be **defined** as a series of relations between primary vowels by which alone the stems of a strong verb are differentiated. There are seven classes of strong verbs in OE., distinguished from one another by the graded vowels of the four stems. The following table shows these vowels in what may be called

## GRADATION-ROWS.

| Class | Pres. | Past Sing. | Past Plur. | Past Part. |
|---|---|---|---|---|
| I. ("Shine") | ī | ā | i | i |
| II. ("Creep") | ēo (ū) | ēa | u | o |
| IIIa. ("Help") | e, eo | ea | u | o |
| b. ("Drink") | i | ǫ | u | u |
| IV. ("Bear") | e | æ | ǣ | o |
| V. ("Tread") | e | æ | ǣ | e |
| VI. ("Fare") | a | ō | ō | a |
| VII. (Redupl.) | {ā, ǣ, ēa, ēa, ǫ, ŏ} | ēo, ē | ēo, ē | same as pres. |

NOTES. (1) **NB.** The past sing. and plur. of the 7th Class were originally formed by Reduplication of the root-syllable

§ 70                         VERBS.                         69

(cp. Lat. *do, dedi*; Gk. δίδωμι, δέδωκα), in some verbs with, in others without, gradation. Since the traces of the original reduplication are very few in OE., it is best for the present to rank Class VII. with the other gradation-classes, whilst retaining the name "Reduplicating."

(2) It will be noticed that only in Classes II., IIIa., and IV. are there *four different stems*; that in Classes I., IIIb., and V. there are *three different stems*, and that in Classes VI. and VII. there are only *two different stems*. Nevertheless, excluding past parts. (which cannot be mistaken for any other part), *no pres. form of a strong verb has the same root-vowel as any past form of the same verb.*

(3) The importance of the gradation-rows just given can hardly be exaggerated. They are most easily remembered by learning the principal parts of the verb selected as the name of each class (except in Class VII., in which the vowels of the present are various):

| Class | Infin. | Past Sing. | Past Plur. | Past Part. |
|---|---|---|---|---|
| I. ("Shine") | scīnan | scān | scinon | scinen |
| II. ("Creep") | crēopan | crēap | crupon | cropen |
| IIIa. ("Help") | helpan | healp | hulpon | holpen |
| b. ("Drink") | drincan | dronc | druncon | druncen |
| IV. ("Bear") | beran | bær | bǣron | boren |
| V. ("Tread") | tredan | træd | trǣdon | treden |
| VI. ("Fare") | faran | fōr | fōron | faren |

(4) *Given the class* of a strong verb, the gradation-rows, together with the rules of §§ 68, 69, suffice for the complete conjugation of *all perfectly regular* (i.e. the majority of) Old English strong verbs. Irregularities are fully dealt with in their place.

## 71. How to tell the class of a strong verb.

In the gradation-rows as repeated below, the vowels printed **black** are in themselves conclusive (irregularities apart) as to the class of the verbs in which they are found, since they occur nowhere else in strong verbs *in the same parts*[1]; as to those printed in *italic* there is more or less uncertainty, which is removed however by the hints given at the foot.

| Class | Infin. | Past Sing. | Past Plur. | Past Part. |
|---|---|---|---|---|
| I. ("Shine") | ī | ā | i | i |
| II. ("Creep") | ēo, ū | ēa | *u* | *o* |
| IIIa. ("Help") | *e*, eo | ea | *u* | *o* |
| b. ("Drink") | i | ǫ(a) | *u* | u |
| IV. ("Bear") | *e* | *æ* | ǣ | *o* |
| V. ("Tread") | *e* | *æ* | ǣ | e |
| VI. ("Fare") | a | ō | ō | a |
| VII. (Redupl.) | ā, ǣ, ea, ēa, ǫ, ō | ēo, ē | ēo, ē | ā, ǣ, ea, ēa, ǫ, ō |

The only uncertainty therefore lies between Classes II., III., IV. and V., and that is completely dispelled by the following statements:

**The stem-vowel in Classes II. ("Creep") and V. ("Tread")**—between which there is no uncertainty—is followed by a single consonant which is not *l* or *r* (except in past parts. *coren, droren, forloren, froren, hroren*; see § 73).

**The stem-vowel in Class III. is followed by two (or more) consonants, the first of which is a nasal in** (*b*) ("**Drink**"), but not in (*a*) ("**Help**").

**The stem-vowel in Class IV. ("Bear") is followed by *l* or *r* only** (except in *brecan*).

---

[1] It is assumed that *drincan*, e.g., will not be taken for a past plur. or past part. of Class I.

## CLASSES OF STRONG VERBS.

**72. Class I** ("Shine"). Gradation-row: ī ā i i. A regular verb of this class is conjugated in full in § 66. The following are among the commonest verbs of the class; their principal parts are not given here because the student is expected to write them out for himself:

bīdan, *wait*  
bītan, *bite*  
drīfan, *drive*  
gewītan, *depart*  
grīpan, *seize*  
scīnan, *shine*  
sīgan, *sink*  
slītan, *slit*  
stīgan, *ascend, descend*  
swīcan, *cease*.  
wrītan, *write*.

### Irregular.

(*a*) The following verbs come under Verner's Law (see § 169), and accordingly have *d* in place of ð in the past plur. and past part.:

| Infin. | Past Sing. | Past Pl. | Past Part. |
|---|---|---|---|
| līðan, *go* | lāð | lidon | geliden |
| scrīðan, *proceed* | scrāð | scridon | gescriden |
| snīðan, *cut* | snāð | snidon | gesniden |

Whereas Verner's Law fails in

mīðan, *avoid*  
wrīðan, *bind*  
(ā)rīsan, (*a*)*rise*  
gerīsan, *befit*

which therefore retain ð or *s* throughout.

(*b*) For the contracted verbs *lēon, tēon* (accuse), *ðēon, wrēon*, see § 81.

**73. Class II ("Creep").** Gradation-row: ēo, ū ēa u o.
Paradigm: crēopan, crēap, crupon, cropen.

|  | Present | Past |
|---|---|---|
|  | *Indicative.* |  |
| Sing. 1. | crēope | crēap |
| 2. | crīepst | crupe |
| 3. | crīepð | crēap |
| Plur. | crēopað | crupon |
|  | *Subjunctive.* |  |
| Sing. | crēope | crupe |
| Plur. | crēopen | crupen |

*Imperative.*
crēop, crēopað

*Infinitive.*
crēopan, *dat.* -anne

*Participles.*
crēopende                            gecropen

Among the commoner verbs of this class are

| bēodan, *command* | nēotan, *enjoy* |
| brēotan, *break* | scēotan, *shoot* |
| clēofan, *sever* |  |
| drēogan, *endure* | brūcan, *enjoy* |
| flēogan, *fly* | būgan, *bow* |
| flēotan, *float* | dūfan, *dive* |
| gēotan, *pour* | lūcan, *lock* |
| grēotan, *weep* | lūtan, *stoop* |
| hrēowan, *rue* | scūfan, *shove* |
| lēogan, *lie* | slūpan, *glide* |

NOTE. Verbs with *ū* in the present are otherwise perfectly regular: *būgan, bēag, bugon, bogen.*

### Irregular.

(*a*) The following come under Verner's Law (§ 169), with *r* in place of *s*, and *d* in place of ð, in past plur. and past part.:

| | | | |
|---|---|---|---|
| cēosan, *choose* | cēas | curon | gecoren |
| drēosan, *fall* | drēas | druron | gedroren |
| forlēosan, *lose* | forlēas | forluron | forloren |
| frēosan, *freeze* | frēas | fruron | gefroren |
| hrēosan, *fall* | hrēas | hruron | gehroren |
| sēoðan, *seethe* | sēað | sudon | gesoden |

Whereas Verner's Law fails in

ābrēoðan, *fail*                                                      ābroðen

(*b*) For the contracted verbs *flēon, tēon* (draw), see § 81.

**74. Class IIIa ("Help").** Gradation-row: **e, eo ea u o**. Paradigm: helpan, healp, hulpon, holpen.

| | Present | Past |
|---|---|---|
| | *Indicative.* | |
| Sing. 1. | helpe | healp |
| 2. | hilpst | hulpe |
| 3. | hilpð | healp |
| Plur. | helpað | hulpon |
| | *Subjunctive.* | |
| Sing. | helpe | hulpe |
| Plur. | helpen | hulpen |

*Imperative*
help, helpað

*Infinitive.*
helpan, *dat.* -anne

*Participles.*

| | |
|---|---|
| helpende | geholpen |

Among the commoner verbs of this class are:

| | |
|---|---|
| belgan, *be angry* | beorgan, *protect* |
| delfan, *dig* | ceorfan, *carve* |
| meltan, *melt* | feohtan, *fight* |
| swelgan, *swallow* | hweorfan, *turn* |
| swellan, *swell* | meolcan, *milk* |
| sweltan, *die* | steorfan, *die* |
| | weorpan, *throw* |

NOTE. (1) The *ea* of the past sing. is a breaking of *a*, and the *eo* of the pres. is a breaking of *e*. The reason why some verbs have *e* and others *eo* in the present is, that *e* broke before *l* only when followed by *c* or *h* (§ 138).

**Irregular.**

(*a*) Under Verner's Law (§ 169) comes

weorðan, *become*   wearð   wurdon   geworden

(*b*) For the verb *fēolan*, penetrate, see § 81.

(*c*) In three verbs *e* > *ie* after palatal *g* (see § 143):

| | | | |
|---|---|---|---|
| gieldan, *yield, pay* | geald | guldon | gegolden |
| giellan, *yell* | geal(l) | gullon | gegollen |
| gielpan, *boast* | gealp | gulpon | gegolpen |

(*d*) Two verbs have *u* in the pres.:

| | | |
|---|---|---|
| murnan, *mourn* | mearn | murnon |
| spurnan (spornan), *spurn* | spearn | spurnon |

(*e*) Metathesis of *r* is seen in *berstan* < \**brestan*[1] and ðerscan < \**ðrescan*; hence the normal change of *a* to *æ* (see § 100) in the past sing. instead of breaking (§ 136).

| | | | |
|---|---|---|---|
| berstan, *burst* | bærst | burston | geborsten |
| ðerscan, *thresh* | ðærsc | ðurscon | geðorscen |

[1] An asterisk before a word denotes that it is not extant in that form.

(*f*) The root-vowel is not followed by consonants that produce breaking (see § 3) in

| bregdan, *brandish* | brægd | brugdon | gebrogden |
| stregdan, *strew* | strægd | strugdon | gestrogden |

with which may be remembered the anomalous

| frignan, *inquire* | frægn | frugnon | gefrugnen |

NOTES. (2) All these verbs often drop *g* with compensatory lengthening of the preceding vowel (see § 160), thus:

| brēdan (3rd sing. brētt) | brǣd | brūdon | gebrōden |
| frīnan | [frān (Class I.)] | frūnon | gefrūnen |

(3) *Stregdan* is also conjugated weak.

**75. Class IIIb** ("**Drink**"). Gradation-row: i ę u u.
Paradigm: drincan, dronc, druncon, druncen.

|  | **Present** |  | **Past** |
|---|---|---|---|
|  |  | *Indicative* |  |
| *Sing.* 1. | drince |  | dronc |
| 2. | drincst |  | drunce |
| 3. | drincð |  | dronc |
| *Plur.* | drincað |  | druncon |
|  |  | *Subjunctive* |  |
| *Sing.* | drince |  | drunce |
| *Plur.* | drincen |  | druncen |

*Imperative*
drinc, drincað

*Infinitive*
drincan, *dat.* -anne

*Participles*
drincende                   gedruncen

Among the commoner verbs of this class are

| bindan, *bind* | onginnan, *begin* | stincan, *stink* |
| (h)linnan, *cease* | sincan, *sink* | swimman, *swim* |
| limpan, *happen* | singan, *sing* | winnan, *fight* |

NOTES. (1) The Primitive Germanic gradation-row of Class III was **e a u u**. The divergences from this of the English sub-classes "Help" and "Drink" are due to changes which took place partly in Germanic and partly in OE. (i) Germanic *e* > *i* before nasal + consonant: cp. *drincan* and *helpan*. (ii) Germanic *u* > *o* in strong past parts., *except* before nasal + consonant: cp. *geholpen*, *gedruncen*. (iii) OE. *a* > *ǫ* before a nasal (see § 149), and > *ea* (breaking) before *r*, *l*, *h* + consonant: cp. *drǫnc*, *healp*. (iv) See § 74, Note (1).

(2) Double consonants are usually simplified when final: *swimman*, past sing. *swǫm(m)*, imperat. sing. *swim*.

### Irregular.

(*a*) Metathesis of *r* is seen in *bi(e)rnan (beornan)* < **brinnan* and *i(e)rnan* < *rinnan* (extant in *tōrinnan*).

| | | | |
|---|---|---|---|
| bi(e)rnan (beornan), *burn* | bǫrn, barn | burnon | geburnen |
| i(e)rnan, *run* | ǫrn, arn | urnon | geurnen |

(*b*) *Findan* has quasi-weak past sing. *funde* as well as *fǫnd*.

(*c*) For *bringan* see § 90, and for -ðungon, -ðungen, § 80, N. 6.

### 76. Class IV ("Bear").

Gradation-row: e æ ǣ o.
Paradigm: beran, bær, bǣron, geboren.

|  | Present | Past |
|---|---|---|
|  | *Indicative.* |  |
| Sing. 1. | bere | bær |
| 2. | bir(e)st (bierst) | bǣre |
| 3. | bir(e)ð (bierð, § 140) | bær |
| Plur. | berað | bǣron |
|  | *Subjunctive.* |  |
| Sing. | bere | bǣre |
| Plur. | beren | bǣren |
|  | *Imperative.* |  |
|  | ber, berað |  |
|  | *Infinitive.* |  |
|  | beran, *dat.* -anne |  |
|  | *Participles.* |  |
|  | berende | geboren |

The only important verbs of this class are

brecan, *break*  helan, *conceal*  teran, *tear*
cwelan, *die*  stelan, *steal*

**Irregular.**

(*a*) *Scieran*, shear, cut, has diphthongised the vowels of the first three parts, *e > ie, æ > ea, ǣ > ēa*, under the influence of palatal *sc* (see § 143); but *scær, scǣron*, are also found in poetry:

scieran     scear (scær)     scēaron (scǣron)     gescoren

(*b*) Especially important are

cuman, *come*  c(w)ōm  c(w)ōmon  (ge)cumen (cymen)
niman, *take*  nōm (nam)  nōmon (nāmon)  genumen.

NOTE. The ō of the past sing. is borrowed from the past plur., perhaps on the analogy of Class VI. For the other vowels see §§ 146, 148.

**77. Class V ("Tread").** Gradation-row: e æ ǣ e. Paradigm: tredan, træd, trǣdon, treden.

|  | Present | Past |
|---|---|---|
|  | *Indicative.* |  |
| Sing. 1. | trede | træd |
| 2. | tritst | trǣde |
| 3. | trit(t) | træd |
| Plur. | tredað | trǣdon |
|  | *Subjunctive.* |  |
| Sing. | trede | trǣde |
| Plur. | treden | trǣden |
|  | *Imperative.* |  |
|  | tred, tredað |  |
|  | *Infinitive.* |  |
|  | tredan, *dat.* -anne |  |
|  | *Participles.* |  |
|  | tredende | getreden |

The only important verbs of this class are

  drepan, *strike*      sprecan, *speak*
  metan, *mete, measure*    wegan, *carry*
    wrecan, *avenge*

### Irregular.

(*a*) Under Verner's Law (§ 169) come

| | | | |
|---|---|---|---|
| cweðan, *say* | cwæð | cwædon | gecweden |
| wesan, *be* | wæs | wæron (§ 96) | |

Whereas the law fails in

| | | | |
|---|---|---|---|
| (ge)nesan, *survive* | (ge)næs | (ge)næson | genesen |
| lesan, *collect* | læs | læson | gelesen |

(*b*) Diphthongisation due to palatal *g* is seen in all parts of

| | | | |
|---|---|---|---|
| giefan, *give* (§ 143) | geaf | gēafon | gegiefen |
| -gietan, *get* | -geat | -gēaton | -gieten |

(*c*) *Etan* and its compound *fretan* have ǣ in past sing.:

| | | | |
|---|---|---|---|
| etan, *eat* | ǣt | ǣton | geeten |
| fretan, *devour* | frǣt | frǣton | freten |

(*d*) For the **weak presents** biddan, fricgan, licgan, sittan, ðicgan, see § 80, and for the **contracted** verbs gefēon, plēon, sēon, see § 81.

**78. Class VI** ("Fare"). Gradation-row: **a ō ō a**.
Paradigm: faran, fōr, fōron, faren.

| | Present | Past |
|---|---|---|
| | *Indicative.* | |
| Sing. 1. | fare | fōr |
| 2. | færst | fōre |
| 3. | færð | fōr |
| Plur. | farað | fōron |
| | *Subjunctive.* | |
| Sing. | fare | fōre |
| Plur. | faren | fōren |

*Imperative.*
far, farað

*Infinitive.*
faran, *dat.* -anne

*Participles.*
farende                             gefaren

The more important verbs of this class are

bacan, *bake*          galan, *sing*          hladan, *lade*
dragan, *dray*         grafan, *dig*          sacan, *quarrel*

**Irregular.**

(*a*) Diphthongisation after palatal *sc* (§ 144) is frequent in
sc(e)acan, *shake*     scōc, scēoc     scōcon, scēocon     gesc(e)acen

(*b*) The weak verb *wæcnan* supplies the place of the lost pres.
\**wacan* :

[wæcnan], *awake*     wōc          wōcon

(*c*) In two verbs *a* > *ǫ* before *n* (§ 149):

spǫnan, *allure*     spōn     spōnon     gespǫnen
stǫndan, *stand*     stōd     stōdon     gestǫnden

NOTE. The later past of *spǫnan* is *spēon*, **Class VII.**, to which class
*weaxan* ( < \**wahsan*), grow, went over entirely.

(*d*) In several past parts. of this class mutated and unmutated forms alternate (see § 121):

færen + faren          slęgen, slægen + slagen  } § 80
græfen + grafen        ðwęgen, ðwægen + ðwogen }
hlæden + hladen                  hæfen + hafen  } § 81
sæcen + sacen          scępen          + sceapen}

(*e*) For the **weak presents** *hębban*, *hliehhan*, *scęððan*,
*scieppan*, *stæppan*, *swęrian*, and for the **contracted** verbs *flēan*,
*lēan*, *slēan*, *ðwēan*, see §§ 80, 81.

## 79. Class VII (Reduplicating).

*Infin. and Past Part.*      *Past*

Stem-vowels: ā, ǣ, ea, ēa, ǫ, ō      ēo, ē.

**Paradigms**: feallan, fēoll, fēollon, feallen.
lǣtan, lēt, lēton, lǣten.

|  | Present | | Past | |
|---|---|---|---|---|
| | *Indicative.* | | | |
| Sing. 1. | fealle | lǣte | fēoll | lēt |
| 2. | fielst | lǣtst | fēolle | lēte |
| 3. | fielð | lǣt(t) | fēoll | lēt |
| Plur. | feallað | lǣtað | fēollon | lēton |
| | *Subjunctive.* | | | |
| Sing. | fealle | lǣte | fēolle | lēte |
| Plur. | feallen | lǣten | fēollen | lēten |
| | *Imperative.* | | | |
| | feall, feallað | lǣt, lǣtað | | |
| | *Infinitive.* | | | |
| | feallan, | lǣtan, *dat.* -anne | | |
| | *Participles.* | | | |
| | feallende | lǣtende | gefeallen | gelǣten |

NOTE. (1) The only remnant in EWS. prose of the earlier reduplication in the past tense is seen in *heht* (<\**hehāt*) from *hātan*; but *leolc* from *lācan*, *reord* from *rǣdan*, (*on*)*dreord* from (*on*)*drǣdan*, and *leort* from *lǣtan*, are preserved in poetical or non-WS. texts.

The following are the **chief verbs of this class**. They are divided into two sub-classes according to the vowel of the past tense, and are then grouped according to the vowel of the present.

NB. *All reduplicating verbs have ēo in the past tense,* **except** those with *ǣ* in the present stem, and *hātan*, *lācan*, *scādan*, and *blǫndan* (blend).

§ 79 VERBS.

I. **Past tense in ēo.**

(i) blāwan, *blow*  māwan, *mow*
cnāwan, *know*  sāwan, *sow*
crāwan, *crow*  swāpan, *sweep*
ðrāwan, *throw*

(ii) fealdan, *fold*  wealcan, *roll*
feallan, *fall*  wealdan, *wield*
healdan, *hold*  weallan, *well*
weaxan, *grow*

(iii) bēatan, *beat*  hēawan, *hew*
hlēapan, *leap*

(iv) bọnnan, *summon*  spọnnan, *join*

(v) blōtan, *sacrifice*  hwōpan, *threaten*
blōwan, *bloom*  rōwan, *row*
flōwan, *flow*  spōwan, *succeed*
grōwan, *grow*  swōgan, *sound, swoon*

II. **Past tense in ē.**

(vi) hātan, *command, call*  lācan, *play*
scādan, *divide*

NOTE. (2) Besides scādan, scēd, etc., we find scēadan, gescēaden, with diphthongised vowel after palatal sc (§ 144), and an anomalous past scēad.

(vii) (on)drǣdan, *dread*  rǣdan, *counsel*
lǣtan, *let*  slǣpan, *sleep*

NOTE. (3) Three of these verbs have also weak forms: -drǣdan and slǣpan have the weak pasts -drǣdde, slǣpte, as well as past part. -drǣd(d); while rǣdan, counsel, read, is always weak in WS., except for one occurrence of the past part. rǣden.

W.

**Irregular.**

(*a*) *Gọngan, gẹngan*, go, has past tense *gēong* (*yang*) and *gẹngde*, pp. *gegọngen*. In prose, only *ēode*, the past tense of *gān* (see § 96), is used.

(*b*) For the **weak present** *wēpan*, and the **contracted** verbs *fōn, hōn*, see §§ 80, 81.

(*c*) *Būan*, dwell, pp. *gebūn*, supplies the place of its lost past tense from the weak *būian, būde, gebūd*.

## WEAK PRESENTS.

**80.** In Classes V., VI. and VII. there are a few verbs, otherwise strong, whose presents resemble those of weak verbs (i.e. were originally formed with *j* or *i*). They are

| *Infin.* | *Past Sing.* | *Past Pl.* | *Past Part.* |
|---|---|---|---|
| Class V ("Tread"). | | | |
| biddan, *request* | bæd | bǣdon | gebeden |
| fricgan, *inquire* | | | {gefregen<br>{gefrigen |
| licgan, *lie* | læg | lǣgon | gelegen |
| sittan, *sit* | sæt | sǣton | geseten |
| ðicgan, *take* | ðeah | ðǣgon | geðegen |
| Class VI ("Fare"). | | | |
| hẹbban, *heave* | hōf | hōfon | gehafen |
| hliehhan, *laugh* | hlōh | hlōgon | |
| scẹððan, *injure* | scōd | scōdon | |
| scieppan, *create* | scōp | scōpon | gesceapen |
| stæppan (stẹppan), *step* | stōp | stōpon | gestapen |
| swẹrian, *swear* | swōr | swōron | gesworen |
| Class VII (Redupl.). | | | |
| wēpan, *weep* | wēop | wēopon | gewōpen |

## § 80  VERBS.

Paradigms: biddan, licgan, hębban, swerian, wēpan.

### Present *Indicative.*

| | | | | | |
|---|---|---|---|---|---|
| *Sing.* 1. | bidde | licge | hębbe | swęrie | wēpe |
| 2. | bidest, bitst | lig(e)st | hęf(e)st | swęrest | wēp(e)st |
| 3. | bideð, bit(t) | lig(e)ð (lið) | hęf(e)ð | swęreð | wēp(e)ð |
| *Plur.* | biddað | licgað | hębbað | swęriað | wēpað |

### Present *Subjunctive.*

| | | | | | |
|---|---|---|---|---|---|
| *Sing.* | bidde | licge | hębbe | swęrie | wēpe |
| *Plur.* | bidden | licgen | hębben | swęrien | wēpen |

### Past *Indicative.*

| | | | | | |
|---|---|---|---|---|---|
| *Sing.* 1. | bæd | læg | hōf | swōr | wēop |
| 2. | bǣde | lǣge | hōfe | swōre | wēope |
| 3. | bæd | læg | hōf | swōr | wēop |
| *Plur.* | bǣdon | lǣgon | hōfon | swōron | wēopon |

### Past *Subjunctive.*

| | | | | | |
|---|---|---|---|---|---|
| *Sing.* | bǣde | lǣge | hōfe | swōre | wēope |
| *Plur.* | bǣden | lǣgen | hōfen | swōren | wēopen |

### *Imperative.*

| | | | | | |
|---|---|---|---|---|---|
| *Sing.* 2. | bide | lige | hęfe | swere | wēp |
| *Plur.* 2. | biddað | licgað | hębbað | swęriað | wēpað |

### *Infinitive.*

| | | | | | |
|---|---|---|---|---|---|
| *Dat.* (tō) | biddanne | licganne | hębbanne | swerianne | wēpanne |

### *Participles.*

| | | | | | |
|---|---|---|---|---|---|
| *Pres.* | biddende | licgende | hębbende | sweriende | wēpende |
| *Past.* | gebeden | gelegen | gehafen | gesworen | gewōpen |

NOTES. (1) Like *licgan* are conjugated the presents of *fricgan*, *ðicgan*; and like *biddan* the presents of all the other verbs with double consonants.

(2) The principal parts, as given on p. 82, must be committed to memory, because of their great irregularity and the uselessness of applying §§ 70, 71, to them.

(3) The irregularities of these verbs are all seen in their principal parts. Otherwise, they are conjugated *in the present like regular weak verbs, and in the past like regular strong verbs*.

(4) These verbs may be **recognised as having weak presents in four ways**, which will be best appreciated by comparison with the tests for strong and for weak verbs in § 64:

(i) They have *mutated root-vowels throughout the present*. Strong presents have mutated vowels in the 2nd and 3rd sing. only (§ 68).

(ii) In the majority of them the original vowels, the mutated forms of which are seen in the present, are contained in the past participles. Strong verbs of Classes V., VI., and VII., have the same vowels in the present and in the past participle.

(iii) The original *j*, which is to be traced in the doubled consonants and in the *i* of *swerian* (see Note 5), is a mark of weak presents.

(iv) The imperative sing. in -*e* (except in *wēpan*) is peculiar to weak verbs.

(5) [1]Besides their weak presents, these verbs show several other irregularities. We often meet with the intrusive vowel, to which attention was called in § 34 (6), in *fricg(e)an*, *licg(e)an*, *ðicg(e)an*, *licgeað*, etc. *Swerian* alternates with *swer(i)g(e)an*. It is possible that the past parts. *fregen*, *frigen*, belong to the very irregular verb *frignan* of Class III. *Hlōgon* and *scōdon* come under Verner's Law. Besides *sceððan* there is a strong infin. *sceaðan*, and besides *scōd* a weak past *sceðede*. Diphthongisation after palatal *sc* is seen in *sceaðan*, *gesceapen*, *scēod* (x *scōd*), and *scēop* (x *scōp*). In *scieppan*,

---

[1] If the student is puzzled by this note he will find full explanations in Part II.

this diphthongisation has been followed by mutation (see §123). In *hlịehhan*, the same vowel has resulted from mutation of broken *a*. The vowel in *sẹah*, as in *seah* (§ 80), is a breaking of original *a*. The *o* of *sworen* (<*swaren*), like that of *swogen* (§ 78), is due to the influence of the preceding *w*. The interchange of *bb* and *f* in *hębban* is explained by the fact that *bb* in OE. represents earlier *fj*. The doubled consonants (eg = gg) of the presents stand for earlier consonant +*j*, and thus = the *ri* (= *rj*) of *swęrian*, *r* being the only consonant that was not doubled after a short vowel through influence of following *j*.

## CONTRACTED VERBS.

**81.** All strong verbs whose present stem originally ended in *h*, lose the *h* and contract before every termination beginning with a vowel. In fact *h* remains only before the -*st*, -ð, of the 2nd and 3rd sing. pres., and when final in the 2nd sing. imperative and 1st and 3rd sing. past; it has been replaced by *g* in the pret. plur. (and derived parts) and past part. in accordance with Verner's Law (see § 169).

The chief strong contracted verbs are:

*Class.*

| | | |
|---|---|---|
| **I.** ("Shine") | lēon, *lend* | [1]ðēon, *thrive*[a] |
| | tēon, *accuse* | wrēon, *cover* |
| **II.** ("Creep") | flēon, *flee* | tēon, *draw* |
| **IIIa.** ("Help") | [2]fēolan, *penetrate* | |
| **V.** ("Tread") | gefēon, *rejoice* | sēon, *see* |
| | plēon, *adventure* | |
| **VI.** ("Fare") | flēan, *flay* | slēan, *slay* |
| | lēan, *blame* | ðwēan, *wash* |
| **VII.** (Reduplicating) | fōn, *seize* | hōn, *hang* |

[1] The numbers in brackets refer to the following notes.
[2] Strictly speaking, *fēolan* is not a contracted verb (see § 154), but this is the most convenient place to give its conjugation.

**Paradigms.**

|  | I. téon | II. téon | III. féolan |
|---|---|---|---|
|  |  |  | PRESENT |
| *Sing.* 1. | téo | téo | féole (§ 13) |
| 2. | tīhst[1] | tiehst | fielhst |
| 3. | tīhð | tiehð | fielhð |
| *Plur.* | téoð | téoð | féolað |
|  |  |  | PRESENT |
| *Sing.* | téo | téo | féole |
| *Plur.* | téon | téon | féolen |
|  |  |  | PAST |
| *Sing.* 1. | táh[5] | téah | fealh |
| 2. | tige | tuge | [fǽle] fulge[2] |
| 3. | táh | téah | fealh |
| *Plur.* | tigon | tugon | [fǽlon] fulgon |
|  |  |  | PAST |
| *Sing.* | tige | tuge | [fǽle] fulge |
| *Plur.* | tigen | tugen | [fǽlen] fulgen |
|  |  | *Imperative.* |  |
| *Sing.* 2. | tīh[1] | téoh | feolh |
| *Plur.* 2. | téoð | téoð | féolað |
|  |  | *Infinitive* (dat.). |  |
|  | (tó) téonne | téonne | féolanne |
|  |  | *Participles.* |  |
| *Pres.* | téonde | téonde | féolende |
| *Past.* | tigen | togen | [folen][2] |

## § 81 VERBS.

| V. sēon | VI. slēan | VII. fōn |
|---|---|---|
| *Indicative.* | | |
| sēo | slēan | fō |
| sichst | slichst | fēhst |
| siehð | slichð | fēhð |
| sēoð | slēað | fōð |
| *Subjunctive.* | | |
| sēo | slēa | fō |
| sēon | slēan | fōn |
| *Indicative.* | | |
| seah | slōg[4] | fēng[4] |
| (sǣge) sāwe[3] | slōge | fēnge |
| seah | slōg | fēng |
| (sǣgon) sāwon | slōgon | fēngon |
| *Subjunctive.* | | |
| (sǣge) sāwe | slōge | fēnge |
| (sǣgen) sāwen | slōgen | fēngen |
| *Imperative.* | | |
| seoh | sleah | fōh |
| sēoð | slēað | fōð |
| *Infinitive* (dat.). | | |
| sēonne | slēanne | fōnne |
| *Participles.* | | |
| sēonde | slēande | fōnde |
| (segen) sewen[3] | (slagen) slægen[3] | fǫngen |

NOTES. (1) The uncontracted vowel of the 2nd and 3rd sing. pres. is a mutation of the uncontracted vowel (broken in Classes III., V., VI.) which is preserved in the imperative sing. This will be better understood when the prehistoric forms of the infinitive are given:

    I.   tēon < *tīhan.

    II.  tēon < *teuhan.

    III. fēolan < *feolhan (breaking) < *felhan.

    V.   sēon < *seh(w)an [3].

          gefēon < *-fehan [3].

    VI. slēan < *slahan.

    VII. fōn < *fōhan.

(2) The past pl. *fulgon* (and derived parts) is rare, and pp. *folgen* is wanting. In their place have been formed a past plur. and pp. according to Class IV ("Bear").

(3) The past plur. and pp. *sǣgon*, *segen*, are necessarily given in the paradigm, because they are the model for the other verbs of the class, but (like pp. *slagen*) they are not the usual forms. As is seen above, the root of *sēon* originally ended in *hw*, which in the past plur. and pp. > *gw* by Verner's Law; *gw* > *g* or *w* in OE., but > *w* in WS. prose. See § 169.

(4) The *g* of the past plur. has been extended to the sing. in Classes VI. and VII. Forms like *slōh* are *later* than *slōg*.

(5) Through the identity of the contracted forms of *tēon* (I.) and *tēon* (II.), the former passed over into Class II. and was followed by *wrēon*, so that we frequently meet with such forms as *tēah*, *tugon*, *wrēah*, *wrogen*, belonging to verbs of Class I.

(6) Connected with ðēon, thrive, are the past plur. ðungon, the pp. ðungen, and the adj. *geðungen*, distinguished, excellent, belonging to Class III., to which class ðēon ( < *ðihan < *ðinhan) itself originally belonged.

## II. WEAK VERBS.

**82.** Weak verbs are divided into four classes:

Class I ("Wean-Ween"), in -*an* and -*ian*, with
    **mutated stem-vowel throughout.**

Class II[1] ("Tell"), in -*an* (list in § 90), with
    **mutated stem-vowel in the present only.**

Class III[1] ("Look"), in -*ian*, with the
    **stem-vowel not mutated.**

Class IV[1] (Mixed), in -*an*; a few verbs conjugated partly like Class I. and partly like Class III. (see list given in § 93).

The principal parts are the infinitive, past singular, and past participle. It is unnecessary to give rules for forming the other parts from them, beyond this: *Follow the paradigms.* For the ways and means of distinguishing weak verbs from strong see § 64.

Weak verbs betray their weakness of character in a certain hesitancy as to the class they belong to and as to the length of their root-syllable, which leads them at times to transfer themselves from one paradigm and class to another. Once decide the paradigm that a weak verb follows and the rest is easy.

---

[1] Sievers does not make a separate class of "Tell" verbs. Hence Class III. (above) = Sievers' Class II., Class IV. (above) = Sievers' Class III.

## Class I ("Wean-Ween").

### 83. Primary paradigms:

(a) Original short stem: węnnan, accustom (wean).

(b) Original long stem: wēnan, suppose (ween).

#### PRESENT Indicative.

| | | | |
|---|---|---|---|
| Sing. | 1. | węnne | wēne |
| | 2. | węnest | wēn(e)st |
| | 3. | węneð | wēn(e)ð |
| Plur. | | węnnað | wēnað |

#### PRESENT Subjunctive.

| | | |
|---|---|---|
| Sing. | węnne | wēne |
| Plur. | węnnen | wēnen |

#### PAST Indicative.

| | | | |
|---|---|---|---|
| Sing. | 1. | węnede | wēnde |
| | 2. | węnedest | wēndest |
| | 3. | węnede | wēnde |
| Plur. | | węnedon | wēndon |

#### PAST Subjunctive.

| | | |
|---|---|---|
| Sing. | węnede | wēnde |
| Plur. | węneden | wēnden |

#### Imperative.

| | | | |
|---|---|---|---|
| Sing. | 2. | węne | wēn |
| Plur. | 2. | węnnað | wēnað |

#### Infinitive.

| | | |
|---|---|---|
| Dat. | (tō) węnnanne | wēnanne |

#### Participles

| | | |
|---|---|---|
| Pres. | węnnende | wēnende |
| Past. | gewęned (*pl.* gewęnede) | gewēned (*pl.* gewēnde) |

§ 83 VERBS. 91

NOTES. (1) As regards terminations, *wennan* is the model of the original conjugation of this class, *the differences being due solely to syncope and apocope of e after an originally long syllable*.

(2) The double consonant of *wennan* is owing to the original *j*, before which every consonant except *r* was doubled after a short vowel, and to which the mutation of the root-vowel throughout this class is also due: **such stems therefore were originally short.** *Gemination is found in all present forms except 2nd and 3rd sing. pres. and sing. imperative; it is absent in all past forms*.

(3) **Like *wēnan* are conjugated original long stems and all polysyllabic stems**; like *wennan*, original short stems. The latter part of this rule, however, has important exceptions, as will be seen in the following sections.

(4) In words like

| | |
|---|---|
| āfierran, *withdraw* | mierran, *mar* |
| cennan, *bring forth* | pyffan, *puff* |
| cierran, *turn* | stillan, *still* |
| clyppan, *embrace* | ðryccan, *oppress* |
| cyssan, *kiss* | wemman, *defile* |
| fyllan, *fill* | yppan, *reveal* |

the double consonant is original (not a gemination before *j*), and therefore they are original long stems[1] and are conjugated like *wēnan*.

(5) *Ciegan*, call, in which the *g* = original *j*, is also conjugated like *wēnan*: past *ciegde*, pp. *gecieged*.

(6) An occasional imperative sing. in -*e* is met with in long stems: *lǣre* = *lǣr*, *sende* = *send*.

---

[1] It must always be borne in mind that a syllable ending in two consonants is long.

**84. Secondary paradigms**: nerian, *save*; gierwan, *prepare*; swebban, *put to sleep*; settan, *set*; lecgan, *lay*.

### Present *Indicative.*

| | | | | | |
|---|---|---|---|---|---|
| *Sing.* 1. | nerie | gierwe | swebbe | sette | lecge |
| 2. | nerest | gierest | swefest | set(e)st | leg(e)st |
| 3. | nereð | giereð | swefeð | sett | leg(e)ð |
| *Plur.* | neriað | gierwað | swebbað | settað | lecgað |

### Present *Subjunctive.*

| | | | | | |
|---|---|---|---|---|---|
| *Sing.* | nerie | gierwe | swebbe | sette | lecge |
| *Plur.* | nerien | gierwen | swebben | setten | lecgen |

### Past *Indicative.*

| | | | | | |
|---|---|---|---|---|---|
| *Sing.* 1. | nerede | gierede | swefede | sette | legde |
| 2. | neredest | gieredest | swefedest | settest | legdest |
| 3. | nerede | gierede | swefede | sette | legde |
| *Plur.* | neredon | gieredon | swefedon | setton | legdon |

### Past *Subjunctive.*

| | | | | | |
|---|---|---|---|---|---|
| *Sing.* | nerede | gierede | swefede | sette | legde |
| *Plur.* | nereden | giereden | swefeden | setten | legden |

### *Imperative.*

| | | | | | |
|---|---|---|---|---|---|
| *Sing.* 2. | nere | giere | swefe | sete | lege |
| *Plur.* 2. | neriað | gierwað | swebbað | settað | lecgað |

### *Infinitive.*

| | | | | | |
|---|---|---|---|---|---|
| *Dat.* (tō) | nerianne | gierwanne | swebbanne | settanne | lecganne |

### *Participles.*

| | | | | | |
|---|---|---|---|---|---|
| *Pres.* | neriende | gierwende | swebbende | settende | lecgende |
| *Past.* | genered | gegier(w)ed | geswefed | geset(t) | gelegd, -lēd |
| *pl.* | generede | gegierede | geswefede | gesette | gelegde |

NOTE. All these verbs, except *gierwan* (which is conjugated like a short stem), were originally short stems. *Settan* and *lecgan* have conformed to the conjugation of *wenan* in the syncope of medial *e*. The conjugation of *nęrian*, *gierwan* and *swębban* differs from that of *węnnan* only in this: that wherever *węnnan* simplifies *nn* to *n*, *swębban* simplifies *bb* to *f*, *nęrian* drops *i*, and *gierwan* drops *w*.

**85. Nęrian.**—*R* alone has not doubled before *j* after a short vowel. Like *nęrian* (§ 84) then are conjugated

 derian, *injure*    gebyrian, *pertain*
 erian, *plough* (*ear*)   spyrian, *inquire*
 ferian, *carry*    styrian, *stir*
 herian, *praise*
 werian, *defend*

Moreover, verbs with stem-final *l*, *m*, *n*, *s*, *ð*, have passed over from *węnnan* to *nęrian* even in EWS., so that we may also conjugate like the latter

 behelian, *conceal*    trymian (+ trymman), *confirm*
 gremian (+ gremman), *provoke*   ðenian (+ ðennan), *stretch*
 lemian, *oppress*    hrisian (+ hrissan), *shake*
 temian, *tame*    wreðian, *support*

This reduces the verbs conjugated exactly like *węnnan* to a very few, such as

 cnyssan, *knock*    fremman, *perform*
 dynnan, *resound*    hlynnan, *resound*

in addition to *gremman*, etc., already given.

Later, all the verbs mentioned in this §, tend to pass over into Class III ("Look"), so that we find *fremian*, *wenian*; past *fremode*, *trymode*, and so on.

NOTE. Besides *nęrian* we find *nergan*, *nerigan*, *nerigean*, *nerige*, etc., but these probably show mere graphic variants of *i* (= *j*) before *a* and *e*.

**86. Gierwan, swębban, sęttan, lęcgan** (§ 84).

(i) *Gierwan.* Like this verb are conjugated

sierwan, *deceive*    smierwan, *anoint*    wielwan, *roll*

NOTE. (1) In LWS., besides passing over to Class III ("Look"), *sierian*, etc., these verbs were sometimes conjugated with *w* throughout and sometimes without *w* throughout, no two verbs being alike.

(ii) *Swębban.* For $bb < f + j$ cp. *hębban*, § 80. Later, this verb also passed over into Class III ("Look"), *swęfian, swęfode*, etc.

(iii) *Sęttan.* Like *sęttan* are conjugated all weak verbs ending in *-ttan*, e.g.:

    hwęttan, *whet*            ondettan, *confess*
    lęttan, *hinder*           ōnettan, *hasten*
    līcettan, *simulate*       sārettan, *grieve*

NOTES. (2) Verbs in *-ddan*, like *hręddan*, rescue, syncopate like *sęttan* in their past forms: *hrędde, gehrędd*.

(3) The polysyllables retain the *tt* in the sing. imperative: *ōnette*.

(iv) *Lęcgan.* Like *lęcgan* is conjugated *węcgan*, agitate, as regards the simplification of *cg* to *g*; but past *węgede*, etc.

**87. 2nd and 3rd Sing. Present:** *Rules for Classes I. and II.*

(1) **Syncope** of *e* is usual in original long stems; in original short stems only after *c*, *s* and *t*, and occasionally after *l* and *g*. Exs.: *wēnest + wēnst, wēneð + wēnð, dǣleð + dǣlð*; *cnys(e)ð* from *cnyssan, sętt* from *sęttan, ręcð* from *ręccan, węcð* from *węccan*; *sęleð + sęlð, lęgeð + lęgð*.

(2) **Consonant-change** in consequence of syncope takes place according to the rules laid down in § 69, whenever the conditions there specified are present. Exs.: (*hwęteð >*) *hwętt* from *hwęttan*; *fylleð > fylð* from *fyllan*; *cȳðeð > cȳð(ð)* from *cȳðan*; *lǣdest > lǣtst, lǣdeð > lǣt(t)* from *lǣdan*; *hȳdeð > hȳt(t)* from *hȳdan*; *forieldeð > forielt* from *forieldan*; *węndeð > węnt* from *węndan*, and so on.

§ 88                    VERBS.                    95

**88. Past Tense.**—Verbs that form their past tense by adding -de immediately to the root-syllable (including therefore all original long stems; see § 83) are subject to the following rules:

(1) Double stem-finals are simplified: āfierran, āfierde; cęnnan, cęnde; fyllan, fylde.

(2) After a voiceless stem-final, c, p(p), t, s, ff, ss, -de > -te:

|  | Past |  | Past |
|---|---|---|---|
| dręncan, *give to drink* | dręncte | slǣpan, *sleep* | slēpte |
| dyppan, *dip* | dypte | mētan, *find* | mētte |
| līexan, *shine* | līexte | pyffan, *puff* | pyfte |
| cyssan, *kiss* | cyste |  |  |

(3) After a consonant **-dde > -de** and **-tte > -te**:

| ǫndwyrdan, *answer* | ǫndwyrde | āwēstan, *lay waste* | āwēste |
|---|---|---|---|
| sęndan, *send* | sęnde | fæstan, *fasten* | fæste |

(4) ðd > dd in later texts: cȳðan (make known), cȳðde and cȳdde.

(5) Verbs in consonant + l, n, r, should have syllabic l, n, r, in the past, but more frequently they take the ending -ede or -ode:

| seglan, *sail* | seglde | bytlan, *build* | bytlede |
|---|---|---|---|
| ęfnan, *perform* | ęfnde + ęfnede |  |  |
| timbran, *build* | timbrede, timbrode |  |  |

Nęmnan (name) loses n: nęmde (+ nęmnode).

NOTE. Later, these verbs formed presents also according to Class III ("Look"): timbrian, etc.

(6) Apparently in imitation of verbs in Class II., verbs in c sometimes take ht for ct in the past tense and past part.:

|  | Past | PP. |
|---|---|---|
| ōlęcc(e)an, *flatter* | ōlęcte + ōlęhte |  |
| nēalǣc(e)an, *approach* | nēalǣcte + -lǣhte |  |
| īec(e)an, *increase* | īecte + īehte | geīeced + geīeht |
| ðrycc(e)an, *oppress* | ðrycte + ðryhte | geðrycced |

## 89. Past Participle.

(i) *Uninflected.* The uninflected pp. usually ends in *-ed*; but (*a*) after a vowel *-ded* as a rule > *d(d)*, and *-ted* > *t(t)*, while (*b*) after consonant + *d* or *t*, the ending *-ed* was often dropped. Thus we find

(*a*)    tǣlan, *blame*           *pp.* getǣled (+ getǣld)
       nǣtan, *annoy*               genǣt(t)
       tōbrǣdan, *scatter*         tōbrǣd(d)
       lǣdan, *lead*                gelǣd(e)(d)[1]
       geēaðmēdan, *humble*    geēaðmēd(e)(d)[1]
       underðīedan, *subdue*    underðīed(e)(d)[1]

(*b*)    begyrdan, *surround*       begyrd(e)(d)[1]
       scieldan, *shield*           gescield(ed)
       sęndan, *send*              gesend(ed)
       ǫndwyrdan, *answer*       geǫndwyrd
       befæstan, *secure*         befæst
       ātyhtan, *entice*           ātyht

(ii) *Inflected.* In original short stems there is syncope of *e* only after *d, t.* In original long stems, syncope of *e* is usual before a termination beginning with a vowel; but unsyncopated forms are also common, except after *d, t*. After a voiceless consonant *d > t* as in the past tense. Exs.:

| | | Uninflected | Inflected (pl.) |
|---|---|---|---|
| Short | cnyssan, *knock* | gecnysed | gecnysede |
| | sęttan, *set* | gesęt(t) | gesętte |
| Long | fyllan, *fill* | gefylled | gefylde |
| | cȳðan, *make known* | gecȳðed | gecȳðde (later gecȳdde) |
| | nęmnan, *name* | genęmned | genęm(ne)de |
| | besęncan, *immerse* | besęnced | besęncte |
| | āwiergan, *curse* | āwierged | āwierg(e)de |
| | lǣdan, *lead* | gelǣd(e)(d) | gelǣdde |

Of course pps. that syncopate in the uninflected form (nom. sing.) remain syncopated in inflection.

[1] That is, the three extant forms are *geēaðmēded, geēaðmēdd, geēaðmēd*.

## Class II ("Tell").

**90.** A small class of about twenty verbs, with roots ending in c, g, l, originally joined the endings of the past tense and past participle immediately to the root-syllable, i.e. without an intervening i. In consequence, whereas the vowel of the present is mutated, the past forms usually retain the original vowel. Stems ending in c or g had (from the Germanic period) ht in the past tense and past participle. Below are the principal parts of the chief of these verbs, divided into (a) original short stems, (b) original long stems.

|     | *Infin.* | *Past* | *PP.* |
| --- | --- | --- | --- |
| (a) | cwęllan, *kill* | cwealde (§ 137) | gecweald |
|     | sęllan, *give* | sealde | geseald |
|     | stęllan, *place* | stealde | gesteald |
|     | tęllan, *tell* | tealde | geteald |
|     | cwęcc(e)an, *shake* | cweahte (§ 137) | gecweaht |
|     | dręcc(e)an, *vex* | dreahte | gedreaht |
|     | lęcc(e)an, *moisten* | leahte | gelęaht |
|     | ręcc(e)an, *explain* | reahte | gereaht |
|     | stręcc(e)an, *stretch* | streahte | gestreaht |
|     | ðęcc(e)an, *cover* | ðeahte | geðeaht |
|     | węcc(e)an, *wake* | weahte | geweaht |
|     | bycg(e)an, *buy* | bohte (§ 129) | geboht |
| (b) | bepǣc(e)an, *deceive* | bepǣhte | bepǣht |
|     | rǣc(e)an, *reach* | rǣhte | gerǣht |
|     | tǣc(e)an, *teach* | tǣhte | getǣht |
|     | [rēc(e)an >] recc(e)an, *reck* | rōhte |  |
|     | sēc(e)an, *seek* | sōhte | gesōht |
|     | wyrc(e)an, *work* | worhte (§ 129) | geworht |
|     | ðęnc(e)an, *think* | ðōhte (§ 153) | geðōht |
|     | ðync(e)an, *seem* | ðūhte | geðūht |
|     | bręng(e)an, *bring* | brōhte (§ 153) | gebrōht |

98 INFLECTION. § 90

Notes. (1) For the intrusive *e*, so often found wherever *c* or *g* was originally followed by *j*, see § 34, N. 6.

(2) Verbs in *-ecc* frequently borrow the *ę* of the pres. in the past tense and pp., even in EWS.: *lęhte, ręhte, geręht*, etc.

(3) The usual past forms of *bepǣcan, rǣcan, tǣcan*, have borrowed the vowel of the present, but *rāhte, tāhte* and *-tāht* occur in EWS.

(4) For *brengan*, the strong *bringan* (rare pp. *brungen*) of Class IIIb ("Drink"), is more often found.

(5) Occasional pps. according to Class I. are met with, such as *onstęled, getęled*.

(6) It is exceedingly good practice for the student to explain, by the aid of Part II., the relations between the vowels of the present and those of the past forms of these verbs. It is therefore not done for him here, but the following notes may help him in some of the chief difficulties:

*cwęllan* etc.—there is no breaking in OE. before $ll < l+j$ (§ 137).

Sęncan—Sŏhte < *Sāhte < Germanic Sanhta; so *brōhte*.

Ꝥyncan—Ꝥūhte < Germanic Ꝥunhta, with lengthening (as above) in compensation for the loss of the nasal.

**Paradigms:** (*a*) Original short stems, *tęllan*.

(*b*) Original long stems, *sēcan*.

Present *Indicative.*

| | | | |
|---|---|---|---|
| *Sing.* | 1. | tęlle | sēce |
| | 2. | tęl(e)st | sēc(e)st |
| | 3. | tęl(e)ð | sēc(e)ð |
| *Plur.* | | tęllað | sēcað |

Present *Subjunctive.*

| | | |
|---|---|---|
| *Sing.* | tęlle | sēce |
| *Plur.* | tęllen | sēcen |

§ 90 VERBS.

### Past *Indicative.*

| | | | |
|---|---|---|---|
| *Sing.* | 1. | tealde | sōhte |
| | 2. | tealdest | sōhtest |
| | 3. | tealde | sōhte |
| *Plur.* | | tealdon | sōhton |

### Past *Subjunctive.*

| | | |
|---|---|---|
| *Sing.* | tealde | sōhte |
| *Plur.* | tealden | sōhten |

### *Imperative.*

| | | |
|---|---|---|
| *Sing.* 2. | tęle | sēc |
| *Plur.* 2. | tęllað | sēcað |

### *Infinitive.*

| | | |
|---|---|---|
| *Dat.* | (tō) tęllanne | sēcanne |

### *Participles.*

| | | |
|---|---|---|
| *Pres.* | tęllende | sēcende |
| *Past.* | geteald | gesōht |

NOTES. (7) It is obvious that the only important difference between the above paradigms and those of § 83 is in the change of vowel in the past forms of *tęllan* and *sēcan*.

(8) Like *tęllan* are conjugated all the original short stems, i.e. stems with a short vowel followed by a doubled consonant (< consonant + *j*); like *sēcan*, all the original long stems, i.e. those with a long vowel, and those with a short vowel followed by two (different) consonants.

### Class III ("Look").

**91.** The verbs of this class are very numerous; so are those of Class I.; together they outnumber all the other classes, strong and weak. "Look"-verbs all have infinitive in *-ian* (except the few contracted verbs in *-gan = -jan*): the root-vowel is mutated only in the case of a few late formations, from nouns and adjs. with mutated vowels, such as *ęndian*, to end, from *ęnde*, and *grēnian*, to become green, from *grēne*.

**Paradigm**: lōcian, look.

|  | Present | Past |
|---|---|---|
|  | *Indicative.* | |
| Sing. 1. | lōcie | lōcode |
| 2. | lōcast | lōcodest |
| 3. | lōcað | lōcode |
| Plur. | lōciað | lōcedon (-odon) |
|  | *Subjunctive.* | |
| Sing. | lōcie | lōcode |
| Plur. | lōcien | lōcoden |

*Imperative.*
lōca, lōciað

*Infinitive.*
lōcian, *dat.* -anne

*Participles.*
lōciende         gelōcod

NOTES. (1) Note that the *-að*, which in every other class marks the pres. plural, here marks the 3rd sing. pres., while the plural has *-iað*.

(2) The present stems of this class originally ended in *-ōjo*, which did not cause mutation of the root-vowel; hence the rarity of mutated root-vowels in these verbs. The original *j* is preserved not only in the contracted verbs, but in the common variants *ige* for *ie* and *iga*, *igea* for *ia*: *lōcige*, *lōcigen*, *lōcigende*, *lōcig(e)að*, *lōcig(e)an*.

(3) For *-ode*, *-od*, we find less frequently *-ade*, *-ude*, *-ad*, *-ud*, rarely *-ede*, *-ed*; but *-edon* is normal according to § 12.

## 92. Contracted Verbs.

Paradigms: *frēog(e)an*, love; *smēag(e)an*, consider.

### PRESENT Indicative.

| | | | |
|---|---|---|---|
| Sing. | 1. | frēoge | smēage |
| | 2. | frēost | smēast |
| | 3. | frēoð | smēað |
| Plur. | | frēog(e)að | smēag(e)að |

### PRESENT Subjunctive.

| | | |
|---|---|---|
| Sing. | frēoge | smēage |
| Plur. | frēogen | smēagen |

### PAST Indicative.

| | | | |
|---|---|---|---|
| Sing. | 1. | frēode | smēade |
| | 2. | frēodest | smēadest |
| | 3. | frēode | smēade |
| Plur. | | frēodon | smēadon |

### PAST Subjunctive.

| | | |
|---|---|---|
| Sing. | frēode | smēade |
| Plur. | frēoden | smēaden |

### Imperative.

| | | | |
|---|---|---|---|
| Sing. | 2. | frēo | smēa |
| Plur. | 2. | frēog(e)að | smēag(e)að |

### Infinitive.

| | | |
|---|---|---|
| | frēog(e)an | smēag(e)an, smēan |

### Participles.

| | | |
|---|---|---|
| Pres. | frēogende | smēagende |
| Past. | gefrēod | gesmēad |

The following verbs are conjugated

like *frēogan*
  fēogan, *hate*
  tēogan, *ordain*
  twēogan, *doubt*

like *smēagan*
  ðrēagan, *rebuke*

Scōg(e)an, *shoe*, has past *scōde*, pp. *gescōd*.

## Class IV: Mixed Verbs.

**93.** Here belong a few verbs which are conjugated partly like Class I. and partly like Class III. *Fyly(e)an, folgian,* follow, is completely conjugated according to both classes: past *fylgde, folgode,* etc. The four verbs *habban,* have, *libban,* live, *secg(e)an,* say, and *hycg(e)an,* think, are given in full below, with the parts that belong to each class in separate columns.

|  | Class I. | Class III. | Class I. | Class III. |
|---|---|---|---|---|
| | | PRESENT *Indicative.* | | |
| *Sing.* 1. | hæbbe | | libbe | |
| 2. | hæfst | hafast | | liofast |
| 3. | hæfð | hafað | | liofað |
| *Plur.* | ⎰habbað⎱ hæbbað | | libbað | |
| | | PRESENT *Subjunctive.* | | |
| *Sing.* | hæbbe | | libbe | |
| *Plur.* | hæbben | | libben | |
| | | PAST *Indicative.* | | |
| *Sing.* 1. | hæfde | | lifde | |
| 2. | hæfdest | | lifdest | |
| 3. | hæfde | | lifde | |
| *Plur.* | hæfdon | | lifdon | |
| | | PAST *Subjunctive.* | | |
| *Sing.* | hæfde | | lifde | |
| *Plur.* | hæfden | | lifden | |
| | | *Imperative.* | | |
| *Sing.* 2. | | hafa | | liofa |
| *Plur.* 2. | ⎰habbað⎱ hæbbað | | libbað | |
| | | *Infinitive.* | | |
| | habban | | libban | |
| | | *Participles.* | | |
| *Pres.* | hæbbende | | libbende | lifiende |
| *Past.* | gehæfd | | gelifd | |

## § 93 VERBS.

|  | Class I. | Class III. | Class I. | Class III. |
|---|---|---|---|---|

### PRESENT *Indicative.*

| | Class I. | Class III. | Class I. | Class III. |
|---|---|---|---|---|
| *Sing.* 1. | secge | | hycge | |
| 2. | sægst, segst | sagast | hyg(e)st | hogast |
| 3. | sægð, segð | sagað | hyg(e)ð | hogað |
| *Plur.* | secg(e)að | | hycg(e)að | |

### PRESENT *Subjunctive.*

| | | | | |
|---|---|---|---|---|
| *Sing.* | secge | | hycge | |
| *Plur.* | secgen | | hycgen | |

### PAST *Indicative.*

| | Class I. | | Class I. | Class III. |
|---|---|---|---|---|
| *Sing.* 1. | sægde, sæde | (§ 98. 2) | hogde | hogode |
| 2. | sægdest, sædest | | hogdest | hogodest |
| 3. | sægde, sæde | | hogde | hogode |
| *Plur.* | sægdon, sædon | | hogdon | hogedon |

### PAST *Subjunctive.*

| | | | | |
|---|---|---|---|---|
| *Sing.* | sægde, sæde | | hogde | hogode |
| *Plur.* | sægden, sæden | | hogden | hogoden |

### *Imperative.*

| | | | | |
|---|---|---|---|---|
| *Sing.* 2. | sege | saga | | hoga |
| *Plur.* 2. | secg(e)að | | hycg(e)að | |

### *Infinitive.*

| | | | | |
|---|---|---|---|---|
| | secg(e)an | | hycg(e)an | |

### *Participles.*

| | | | | |
|---|---|---|---|---|
| *Pres.* | secgende | | hycgende | |
| *Past.* | gesægd, gesæd | | | gehogod |

NOTES. (1) To Class III. belong originally only the 2nd and 3rd sing. pres. indic. and the 2nd sing. imperative, to Class I. all the other *present* forms. The past was formed by adding *-de*, the past part. by adding *-d*, immediately to the root-syllable, and therefore not strictly on the analogy of any class; but the original past forms are given under Class I., because they closely resemble those of that class.

(2) A negative form of *habban* is formed by prefixing *ne*: *nabban, næfde, genæfd*; which is conjugated throughout like *habban*.

(3) Present forms of *libban* with *fi, fg*, for *bb, lifian, lifgan*, etc., are not uncommon, but are properly dialectal. *Eo* regularly replaces *io* in later forms, *leofað*, etc., and then we have past forms *leofode, geleofod*.

(4) *Īewan*, show, Class I., has also an infin. *īowian*, Class III., and an odd combination of the two *īowan*. The following forms occur in EWS.:

| *Infin.* | īewan | īowian | īowan |
|---|---|---|---|
| 3rd sing. pres. | īew(e)ð | īowað | īoweð |
| 3rd pl. | īewað | īowiað | |
| Subj. pres. | īewe | īowi(g)e | |
| Past. | īewde | (LWS. īowode) | īowde |
| Past part. | geīewed (*pl.* geīewde) | geīowod | |

## 94. How to tell the Class of a Weak Verb.

We are now in a position to tell the class of any weak verb without difficulty (apart from the uncertainty due to verbs of Class I. passing over to Class III., see §§ 85, 86, 88).

(*a*) The verbs of Class II. ("Tell") and Class IV. (Mixed) are all mentioned in §§ 90, 93; the only uncertainty therefore is between Classes I. and III.

(*b*) Verbs in *-an* belong to Class I.;

    „  „ *-ian* „    „    „ III., *except those named in* § 85 (all short stems).

(*c*) Verbs with mutated root-vowel belong to Class I.;

    „  „ unmutated „    „    „ III.;

but a few **long** stems in *-ian* belonging to Class III., such as *endian*, have a mutated vowel as explained in § 91.

### III. PAST-PRESENT VERBS.

**95.** There are twelve verbs in OE. whose **presents are old strong past tenses**, from which new weak past tenses have been formed. Hence they are often called "Preteritive-Present" and also "Strong-Weak" verbs. Their past tenses are conjugated like those of regular weak verbs. Their presents retain two traces of the older conjugation of strong past tenses, in the 2nd

§ 95 VERBS. 105

sing. in -*t* without change of vowel, and in the mutated vowel of the subjunctive (although, through leveling, unmutated vowels occur more frequently). Other present parts, infinitive, imperative, etc., were formed from the past-present plural, but in most of these verbs some parts are missing. Above each verb is stated the *gradation class* to which its past-present belongs, but in some instances there have been changes from the original stem-vowels. Infinitives in square brackets are not found.

|  |  | I ("Shine"). | II ("Creep"). |  | III ("Drink"). |
|---|---|---|---|---|---|
|  |  | *Present Indicative.* | | | |
| *Sing.* | 1. | wāt, *know* | āg (āh), *possess* | dēag (dēah), *avail* | on(n), *grant* |
|  | 2. | wāst | āhst | | |
|  | 3. | wāt | āg (āh) | dēag (dēah) | on(n) |
| *Plur.* |  | witon | āgon | dugon | unnon |
|  |  | *Present Subjunctive.* | | | |
| *Sing.* |  | wite | āge | dyge, duge | unne |
| *Plur.* |  | witen | āgen | dygen, dugen | unnen |
|  |  | *Past Indicative.* | | | |
| *Sing.* | 1. | wiste | āhte | dohte | ūðe |
|  | 2. | wistest | āhtest | dohtest | ūðest |
|  | 3. | wiste | āhte | dohte | ūðe |
| *Plur.* |  | wiston | āhton | dohton | ūðon |
|  |  | *Past Subjunctive.* | | | |
| *Sing.* |  | wiste | āhte | dohte | ūðe |
| *Plur.* |  | wisten | āhten | dohten | ūðen |
|  |  | *Imperative.* | | | |
| *Sing.* | 2. | wite | āge | | (ge)unne |
| *Plur.* | 2. | witað | āgað | | unnað |
|  |  | *Infinitive.* | | | |
|  |  | witan | āgan | dugan | unnan |
|  |  | *Participles.* | | | |
| *Pres.* |  | witende | āgende | dugende | unnende |
| *Past.* |  | (ge)witen | āgen (adj.), *own* | | geunnen |

## INFLECTION.

|  | III ("Drink"). | III ("Help"). | | IV ("Bear"). |
|---|---|---|---|---|

### Present *Indicative*.

| | | | | |
|---|---|---|---|---|
| *Sing.* 1. | cǫn(n), *know (how to)* | dear(r), *dare* | ðearf, *need* | (ge)mǫn, *remember* |
| 2. | cǫnst | dearst | ðearft | (ge)mǫnst |
| 3. | cǫn(n) | dearr | ðearf | (ge)mǫn |
| *Plur.* | cunnon | durron | ðurfon | (ge)munon (-að) |

### Present *Subjunctive*.

| | | | | |
|---|---|---|---|---|
| *Sing.* | cunne | dyrre, durre | ðyrfe, ðurfe | (ge)myne, (ge)mune |
| *Plur.* | cunnen | dyrren, durren | ðyrfen, ðurfen | (ge)mynen, (ge)munen |

### Past *Indicative*.

| | | | | |
|---|---|---|---|---|
| *Sing.* 1. | cūðe | dorste | ðorfte | (ge)munde |
| 2. | cūðest | dorstest | ðorftest | (ge)mundest |
| 3. | cūðe | dorste | ðorfte | (ge)munde |
| *Plur.* | cūðon | dorston | ðorfton | (ge)mundon |

### Past *Subjunctive*.

| | | | | |
|---|---|---|---|---|
| *Sing.* | cūðe | dorste | ðorfte | (ge)munde |
| *Plur.* | cūðen | dorsten | ðorften | (ge)munden |

### *Imperative*.

| | | | | |
|---|---|---|---|---|
| *Sing.* 2. | | | | (ge)mun(e) |
| *Plur.* 2. | | | | (ge)munað |

### *Infinitive*.

| | | | | |
|---|---|---|---|---|
| | cunnan | [durran] | ðurfan | (ge)munan |

### *Participles*.

| | | | | |
|---|---|---|---|---|
| Pres. | | | ðearfende | (ge)munende |
| Past. | {(ge)cunnen<br>{cūð (adj.), *known* | | | (ge)munen |

## § 95 VERBS.

| | IV ("Bear"). | V ("Tread"). | | VI ("Fare"). |
|---|---|---|---|---|

### Present *Indicative*.

| | | IV | V | | VI |
|---|---|---|---|---|---|
| *Sing.* | 1. | sceal, *must* | mæg, *can* | 3rd pers. | mōt, *may* |
| | 2. | scealt | meaht, miht | *only* | mōst |
| | 3. | sceal | mæg | be-, ge-neah, *suffices* | mōt |
| *Plur.* | | sculon, sceolon | magon | -nugon | mōton |

### Present *Subjunctive*.

| | IV | V | | VI |
|---|---|---|---|---|
| *Sing.* | scyle, scule | mæge | -nuge | mōte |
| *Plur.* | scylen, sculen | mægen | -nugen | mōten |

### Past *Indicative*.

| | | IV | V | | VI |
|---|---|---|---|---|---|
| *Sing.* | 1. | sc(e)olde | meahte, mihte | | mōste |
| | 2. | sc(e)oldest | meahtest, mihtest | | mōstest |
| | 3. | sc(e)olde | meahte, mihte | -nohte | mōste |
| *Plur.* | | sc(e)oldon | meahton, mihton | -nohton | mōston |

### Past *Subjunctive*.

| | IV | V | | VI |
|---|---|---|---|---|
| *Sing.* | sc(e)olde | meahte, mihte | -nohte | mōste |
| *Plur.* | sc(e)olden | meahten, mihten | -nohten | mōsten |

### *Imperative.*

*Sing.* 2.
*Plur.* 2.

### *Infinitive.*

| IV | V | | VI |
|---|---|---|---|
| sculan | [magan] | [-nugan] | [mōtan] |

### *Participles.*

*Pres.*
*Past.*

Notes. (1) For *witan*, etc., we find in EWS. *wiotan*, *wietan*, etc. (by *o*-mutation). Another form of the past tenses in EWS. is *wisse*. The negative form of *witan* is *nytan*, with *y* throughout.

(2) *Āgan* has a negative form *nāgan*, *nāh*, etc.

## IV. ANOMALOUS VERBS.

**96.** Four anomalous verbs in OE. are of very frequent occurrence: (*a*) *bēon, wesan*, be; (*b*) *dōn*, do; (*c*) *gān*, go; (*d*) *willan*, will.

(*a*) **Bēon, wesan**, be.

|  | Present |  | Past |
|---|---|---|---|
|  | *Indicative.* | | |
| Sing. 1. | eom | bēo | wæs |
| 2. | eart | bist | wǣre |
| 3. | is | bið | wæs |
| Plur. | sind, sint, si(e)ndon | bēoð | wǣron |
|  | *Subjunctive.* | | |
| Sing. | sīe | bēo | wǣre |
| Plur. | sīen | bēon | wǣren |
|  | *Imperative.* | | |
|  | wes, wesað | bēo, bēoð | |
|  | *Infinitive.* | | |
|  | wesan | bēon, *dat.* bēonne | |
|  | *Participles.* | | |
|  | wesende | bēonde | *wanting* |

NOTES. (1) The forms of this verb beginning with a vowel and all the past tense are compounded with *ne*, not: *neom, nis, næs, nǣron*, etc.

(2) The *-m* of *eom* is almost the sole reminder of the fact that all these anomalous verbs once belonged to the class of verbs in *-mi* (cp. Greek ἐμμί, τίθημι).

(3) The above verb is from three distinct roots: the forms beginning with *b* from one, those with *w* from a second, and all the others from a third.

## § 96 VERBS.

(b) **Dôn**, do.

|  | Present | Past |
|---|---|---|
|  | *Indicative.* |  |
| Sing. 1. | dô | dyde |
| 2. | dêst | dydest |
| 3. | dêð | dyde |
| Plur. | dôð | dydon |

*Subjunctive.*

| Sing. | dô | dyde |
| Plur. | dôn | dyden |

*Imperative.*
dô, dôð

*Infinitive.*
dôn, *dat.* dônne

*Participles.*
dônde — gedôn


(c) **Gán**, go.

*Indicative.*

| Sing. 1. | gá | ĕode |
| 2. | gǽst | ĕodest |
| 3. | gǽð | ĕode |
| Plur. | gáð | ĕodon |

*Subjunctive.*

| Sing. | gá | ĕode |
| Plur. | gán | ĕoden |

*Imperative.*
gá, gáð

*Infinitive.*
gán, *dat.* gánne

*Participles.*
gánde — gegán

NOTE. (4) With this verb cp. the reduplicating verb *gongan* (§ 79), with which it is synonymous.

(d) **Willan**, will.

|  | Present |  | Past |
|---|---|---|---|
|  |  | *Indicative.* |  |
| Sing. 1. | wille, wile |  | wolde |
| 2. | wilt |  | woldest |
| 3. | wile, wille |  | wolde |
| Plur. | willað |  | woldon |
|  |  | *Subjunctive.* |  |
| Sing. | wil(l)e |  | wolde |
| Plur. | willen |  | wolden |
|  |  | *Imperative.* |  |
| Plur. 2. | [nyllað, nellað] |  |  |
|  |  | *Infinitive.* |  |
|  | willan |  |  |
|  |  | *Participle.* |  |
|  | willende |  |  |

NOTE. (5) *Willan* unites with *ne* to form a negative verb, which has *y* or *e* for *i* throughout the present: nyl(l)e, nel(l)e, nolde, etc. In WS. no imperative is found but the negative plural.

# PART II. PHONOLOGY.

**97.** In this Part the attempt is made to give such an account of the principal sound-changes that took place between the Germanic period and the end of the Old English period, as will suffice for the intelligent comprehension of the Accidence in Part I. While no difficulty has been shirked, it goes without saying that many difficulties are excluded from the scope of an elementary text-book. The limits and order of exposition adopted it will be convenient to state succinctly here. Attention is given almost exclusively to the vowels of stressed syllables; the vowels of unstressed syllables are included only so far as they are essential to the understanding of the changes in stressed vowels; a few paragraphs are devoted to the most important changes in consonants. No more is said about changes that took place between Indo-Germanic and Germanic (see the table, § 1), or during the Germanic period, than is necessary for the explanation of subsequent changes. A few developments manifested after the Early West Saxon period are mentioned for the sake of completeness, but in each case it is clearly indicated that they are late.

The order of exposition is this: (*a*) Starting with the Germanic system of stressed vowels, we find the normal equivalent of each vowel-sound in OE., which gives us the series of OE primary vowels (§§ 100—112). These are then included in a comparative table with those of other Germanic languages

(§ 113). (b) The sound-changes, which produced the secondary or derivative vowels, are next dealt with separately, and examples given under each head (§§ 114—62). (c) The upward history of each OE. stressed vowel and diphthong, both primary and secondary, is given in tabular form (§ 163). (d) The principal phenomena seen in the development of the OE. consonants are briefly set forth (§§ 164—9).

## STRESSED VOWELS.

### A DOWNWARD HISTORY.—OE. Primary Vowels.

**98.** At the close of the Germanic period, i.e. before the death of the parent language in giving birth to dialects which became the Germanic languages, the system of stressed vowels was as follows:

[1]a, e, i[(1)], o[(2)], u;  ā[(3)], ǣ, ē, ī[(4)], ō, ū[(4)];   ai, au, eu (iu[(5)]).

NOTES. (1) This *i* includes, not only original *i*, but the *i* that arose from *e* in the Germanic period, (a) before nasal + consonant, whence the difference of vowel in OE. *drincan* and *helpan* belonging to the same class of strong verbs; (b) before *i* or *j* in the same or the next syllable, whence the difference of vowel in OE. *biddan* (< *bedjan*) and the past part. *gebeden*.

(2) Germanic had lost original *o*, as may be seen by a comparison of Lat. *hortus* with Gothic *gards*, Eng. *yard*. Every Germanic *o* in stressed syllables, then, had arisen during the Germanic period in accordance with the following important law. Earlier Germanic *u* > *o* under the influence of original *o* or *a* in the next syllable; but if (a) nasal + consonant or (b) *i* or *j* intervened, *u* was protected from change. This law has the most marked and important bearings on OE. phonology. Thus, on (a) depends the difference between such OE. past parts. as *gedruncen* (Class 3b) and all strong past parts. with root-vowel *o* (Classes 2, 3a, 4). For the vowel of the ending -*en* was *a* in Germanic, and this, according to the law, caused the change *u* > *o* in all strong past parts. where *u* was not protected by nasal + consonant. Again, on a knowledge of (b) depends the understanding of OE. *i*-mutation. For whereas in OE. *gold*, being an *o*-stem, the original *u* of the root > *o* in Germanic under the influence of the following *o*; in the derivative adjective

---

[1] The numbers in brackets refer to the notes.

*gylden*, the original *i* of the ending *-en* (< *iu*) protected the *u* of the root from change until the period of the OE. *i*-mutation.

(3) Similarly, Germanic had lost original *ā*, as may be seen by comparing Lat. *frāter* with OE. *brōðor*. Every Germanic *ā* in stressed syllables had arisen in the Germanic period from $a + nh$ which $> ā + h$, with compensatory lengthening for the loss of the nasal. Thus Germanic *ā* is found only before *h*.

(4) In the same way Germanic $i + nh > ī + h$,

and ,, $u + nh > ū + h$;

but, unlike *ā*, these are not the only *ī* and *ū* in Germanic.

(5) Germanic *iu* < *eu*, just as *i* < *e*, before *i* or *j*. Hence no Germanic *e* or *eu*, but *i* and *iu*, came down to prehistoric OE. *iu* words in which there was originally a following *i* or *j*.

**99.** The West Germanic (see § 1) system of stressed vowels differed in only one particular from that of Germanic:

Germanic *ā* > West Germanic *ā*,

but ,, *ǣ* > ,, ,, *ā*.

Apart from this last vowel, it is immaterial whether we make Germanic or West Germanic the point from or to which we trace the OE. vowels. In dealing with this particular vowel due care must be taken. With this caution we proceed to trace seriatim the normal developments of the Germanic vowels as given in § 98. It must be borne in mind that *all changes in stressed vowels that come under the special phenomena dealt with in § 114 foll. are excluded from §§ 100—13.*

**100.** (West) Germanic **a** > (*a*) OE. **a**, (*b*) OE. **æ**.

(*a*) OE. **a** is found, i.e. Germanic *a* remains, in open syllables (i.e. before a single consonant) followed by a guttural vowel (a, o, u) or by an *e* or *i* weakened from *o* or *u*: *faran*, to go, and the other verbs of the 6th strong class; *gafol*, tax; *laðung*, invitation; *laðian* (i < ō), invite.

Notes. (1) OE. *a* is rarely found in closed syllables: *habban*; *nabban*; *appla*, plur. of *æppel*, apple; *assa*, ass; *asce*, ashes; and a few less common words.

(2) OE. *a* is always found in the imperative sing. of strong verbs of Class 6 : *far* from *faran*.

(*b*) In most other instances—apart from the special influences and sound-changes which are dealt with in § 114 foll.—**a** > **æ**. This must be regarded as the normal development, just as that of *ā* is to *ǣ*. It is the rule in closed syllables, and before an *e* which is not weakened from *o* or *u* : *dæg*, day ; *fæt*, vessel ; *blæc*, black ; *bær*, *træd*, and the other past sings. of the 4th and 5th strong classes ; hence in *mæg*, can, a "past-present" of the 5th class ; *bræyd*, past of *bregdan*, brandish (§ 74, c. f.) ; *dæges*, *dæge*, etc. : *fæder* (e < a) ; *æcer*, field ; *fæger*, fair.

NOTE. (3) OE. *æ* is steadfast in the gen. and dat. sing. of masc. and neuter nouns of the ordinary declension, such as *dæg*, *fæt*, above ; but in all other flexional forms of nouns and verbs where *æ* would be normal, *a* is carried over from forms where *a* is normal : *hwate*, instrumental masc. and neut. sing. and nom. acc. masc. pl. of *hwæt*, active ; *hwates*, gen. sing. masc. and neuter, on the analogy of *hwatu*, *hwata*, *hwatum* ; so *fare*, *faren*, *farende*, following *faran*, etc.

**101.** (W.) Germ. **e** often remains in OE. ; e.g. in many verbs of the 3rd, 4th and 5th strong classes, such as *helpan*, *beran*, *brecan*, *tredan*, pp. *getreden*; and in *feld*, field ; *helm*, helmet ; *weg*, way, etc.

**102.** (W.) Germ. **i** (see § 98, Note 1) often remains in OE. ; e.g. in the past plural and past part. stems of strong verbs of the 1st Class : *scine*, *scinon*, *gescinen*, etc.; in the prons. *ic*, *inc*, *hit* ; in the "past-present" verb *witan*; in *is*, is ; in *fisc*, fish ; *micel*, great, etc.; in verbs of the strong Class IIIb ("Drink") : *drincan*, *winnan*, fight, etc. ; in *blind*, blind ; in the 2nd and 3rd sing. of strong verbs of the 3rd, 4th and 5th Classes : *hilpst*, *hilpð* from *helpan* ; *bir(e)st*, *bir(e)ð* from *beran* ; *itst*, *itt* from *etan* ; and in "weak presents" of the 5th Class of strong verbs : *biddan*, ask ; *sittan*, etc.

NOTES. (1) (W.) Germ. *i* has weakened to *e* in *mec*, me, and in several other pronominal forms in which the *e* was subsequently lengthened, e.g. *mē*, to me, me (see § 161).

(2) OE. *i* is replaced by *y* (sometimes *e*) in the negative forms of *witan* and *willan*, *nytan*, *nyllan* (*nellan*), etc., and occasionally in other words, especially in LWS. Cp. the replacement of EWS. *ie* by LWS. *y* (§ 116).

**103.** (W.) Germ. **o** (see § 98, N. 2) usually remains in OE.; e.g. in past parts. of Classes II., IIIa. and IV. of strong verbs: *geboden*, *geholpen*, *geboren*; and in

| | | |
|---|---|---|
| gold, *gold* | wolc(e)n, *cloud* | folgian, *to follow* |
| scop, *bard* | scotung, *shot* | ofer, *over* |
| corn, *corn* | | |

and many other words.

NOTE. (W.) Germ. *o* > *u* in a number of words, e.g.

| | | |
|---|---|---|
| duru, *door* | wull, *wool* | lufian, *to love* |
| fugol, *bird* | bucca, *buck* | cnucian, *to knock* |
| full, *full* | rust, *rust* | ufan, *above* |
| lufu, *love* | wulf, *wolf* | furðor, *further* (cp. forð) |

For this change no reason has been assigned.

**104.** (W.) Germ. **u** often remains; e.g. in past plurals of the 2nd and 3rd Classes of strong verbs: *budon*, *hulpon*, *druncon*; in past parts. of Class IIIb.: *gedruncen*; and in

| | | |
|---|---|---|
| sunu, *son* | hungor, *hunger* | unc, (*to*) *us two* |
| grund, *ground* | burg, *stronghold* | lungre, *quickly* |

NOTE. (W.) Germ. *u* > *o* in the stressed prefix *or-* (out of, without); e.g.

| | |
|---|---|
| orlęge, *war* | orsorg (= Lat. *se-curus*) |
| ordęnc, *skill* | ormōd, *despondent* |

**105.** Germ. **ǣ** = W. Germ. *ā* (§ 99) > (*a*) OE. **ā**, (*b*) usually OE. **ǣ**.

(*a*) OE. *ā* is found, i.e. W. Germ. *ā* remains, (1) before *w*: e.g. the past plural etc. of *sēon*, *sāwon*; *clāwu* (claw), *tāwian* (prepare), and the foreign word *pāwa* (peacock). (2) In an open syllable before a guttural vowel, interchanging with *ǣ*: *slāpan* ∝ *slǣpan*, to sleep; *lāgon* ∝ *lǣgon*, past pl. of *licgan*; *lācnian* ∝ *lǣcnian* (i < ō), to heal; *māgas* ∝ *mǣgas*, *māgum* ∝ *mǣgum*, pl. of *mǣg*, kinsman.

(b) OE. (WS.) **ǣ** is the normal development of Germanic *ǣ* through W. Germ. *ā*, just as OE. *æ* is of Germ. *a* (cp. § 100). Examples are seen in the past pls. of strong Classes IV. and V.: *bǣron, trǣdon*; in some Reduplicating verbs, *lǣtan*, etc.; in the privative prefix *ǣ-*, e.g. *ǣmen*, uninhabited; and in *rǣd* ('rede'), *wǣpn* (weapon), *strǣt* (< L. strāta), etc.

NOTE. Germanic *ā* (§ 98, N. 3) > OE. *ō*; but as this is in reality a case of nasal influence it is dealt with in § 152.

**106.** (W.) Germ. **ē** is the only letter that passed into English without undergoing any change. It is of comparatively rare occurrence. Exs.: *hēr*, here; *mēd*, reward; and past tenses in *ē* of Reduplicating verbs: *lēt, slēpon*, etc. (Sievers).

**107.** (W.) Germ. **ī** > OE. *ī* in the great majority of instances; e.g. all the present parts of strong verbs of Class I.: *scīnan, scīn, scīnende*, etc.; *oferðīhð* (§§ 81 and 98, N. 4) from *oferðēon* (excel); *līf* (life), *wīs* (wise), *wīsian* (to direct), etc.

**108.** (W.) Germ. **ō** almost always > OE. *ō*; e.g. past tenses of strong verbs of Class VI.: *fōr, fōron*; hence in *mōt* (may), a "past-present" of Class VI.; some Reduplicating verbs:

blōwan, *to bloom*   grōwan, *to grow*   swōgan, *to sound*

and in

dōm, *doom*   ōfost, *haste*   swōte, *sweetly*
wrōht, *accusation*   gōd, *good*   sōhte, *sought*

**109.** (W.) Germ. **ū** almost always remains in OE.; e.g. aorist-presents of the 2nd class of strong verbs: *lūcan* (lock), *būgan* (bow), etc.; *tūn* (enclosure), *fūl* (foul), *rūm* (roomy), *ðūhte* (see § 98, N. 4) from *ðyncan* (seem).

**110.** (W.) Germ. **ai** > OE. **ā** usually; e.g. the past sing. of the 1st class of strong verbs: *stāg* from *stīgan* (ascend), *scān* from *scīnan* (shine); hence in *wāt* (know), *āg* (possess), "past-presents" of Class I.; in some Reduplicating verbs:

| hātan, *command* | lācan, *play* | swāpan, *sweep* |

and in

| stān, *stone* | ān, *one* | mā, *more* |
| sār, *wound* | hāl, *hale* | |

**111.** (W.) Germ. **au** > OE. **ēa** usually; e.g. the past sing. of strong verbs of Class II.: *crēap* from *crēopan* (creep), *cēas* from *cēosan* (choose); hence in *dēag* (avails), a "past-present" of the same class; Reduplicating verbs with root-vowel *ēa*: *bēatan* (beat), *hēawan* (hew), etc.;

| dēað, *death* | hēah, *high* | ēac, *eke* |
| hēafod, *head* | glēaw, *prudent* | ðēah, *though* |
| ēare, *ear* | | |

**112.** (W.) Germ. **eu** > OE. **ēo** (*īo*) invariably; e.g. strong verbs of Class II.:

| crēopan, *creep* | sēoðan, *seethe* | hrēowan, *rue*; |

and

| dēor, *animal* | ðēod, *nation* | getrēow, *true* |
| hrēow, *regret* | dēop, *deep* | sēoc, *sick* |
| lēoht, *light* | | |

alternating with *crīopan, dīor, līoht, ðīod, dīop, sīoc*, etc.

NOTES. (1) (W.) Germ. *eu* occasionally remains unchanged in the oldest texts: ðeuw = ðēow, servant.

(2) (W.) Germ. **iu** arose only before *i* or *j* (see § 98, N. 5), which subsequently caused mutation to *ie* in the OE. period. See § 126.

**113.** The following table shows the normal correspondences between the stressed vowels of Germanic, Gothic, Icelandic, Old High German and Old English. To include in such a table the special developments dealt with in the succeeding paragraphs, especially where they are as numerous as in Icelandic and Old English, would simply be to rob the table of any use it may have.

## NORMAL CORRESPONDENCES OF STRESSED VOWELS.

| Germanic | Gothic | Icelandic | OHG. | OE. |
|---|---|---|---|---|
| a | a | a | a | æ (a) |
| e | i, aí (= ę) | e | e | e |
| i | i, aí (= ę) | i | i | i |
| o | u, aú (= ǫ) | o | o | o |
| u | u, aú (= ǫ) | u | u | u |
| ā (§ 98, N. 3) | ā | ā | ā | ō |
| ǣ (W. Germ. ā) | ē | ā | ā | ǣ (ā) |
| ē | ē | ē | ie | ē |
| ī | ei (= ī) | í | ī | ī |
| ō | ō | ō | uo (ua) | ō |
| ū | ū | ú | ū | ū |
| ai | ái | ei | ei (ē) | ā |
| au | áu | au | ou (ō) | ēa |
| eu (iu) | iu | jō (ȳ) | eo, io (iu) | ēo |

## B. THE OLD ENGLISH SOUND-LAWS.

**114.** Under the above convenient and comprehensive heading it is proposed to trace the chief developments of the Germanic stressed vowels (*apart from the normal correspondences*), which took place in the OE. period, prehistoric and historic. Under this heading are included (*a*) Changes due to following vowels, (*b*) to neighbouring consonants, (*c*) to the loss of consonants: (*d*) Lengthening and Shortening. Following this arrangement the laws of sound-change are considered under the following names:

(*a*)   I.   *I*- or *J*-Mutation (Mut.).

      II.   *U*- or *O*-Mutation (*U*-Mut.).

(*b*)   III.   Palatal Mutation (Mut. Pal.).

      IV.   Breaking (Brk$^g$).

      V.   Glide-Diphthongisation (Glide-Diph.).

      VI.   Palatal Diphthongisation (Pal. Diph.).

      VII.   ,,   Monophthongisation (Pal. Mon.).

      VIII.   Influence of preceding *W* (*W*-Infl.).

      IX.   ,,   following *W* (Infl.-*W*.).

      X.   ,,   ,,   Nasal (Infl.-*N*.).

(*c*)   XI.   Lengthening in compensation for lost Nasal (Loss-*N*).

      XII.   Contraction (Contr.).

      XIII.   Lengthening in compensation for loss of *G* or *H* (Loss-*G*, Loss-*H*).

(*d*)   XIV.   Lengthening (Length$^g$).

      XV.   Shortening (Short$^g$).

The foregoing names (if sometimes clumsy) are *significant*; that is to say, they suggest with sufficient clearness the nature of the processes which they denote. The abbreviations in parentheses are convenient substitutes, especially for the longer names, and frequently save making a reference.

**115.** It is not possible to assign the exact chronological order in which the processes represented above came into operation. Some of them, e.g. Breaking, were completed in prehistoric times, others had hardly manifested themselves at the commencement of the historic OE. period, e.g. $U$-Mutation; some of them must have been in operation over a considerable period of time, e.g. Palatal Mutation. But by careful observation of the processes that precede, and the processes that follow, other processes in the successive sound-changes of the same word, the present writer has formulated the following scheme of **processes in the approximate order of their appearance**, which is probably not very far from the truth. Those on the same level are supposed to be nearly synchronous, but dates are not assigned (for abbreviations see above).

(1)                 Shortening

(2)   Breaking      Contraction          Infl.-$N$

(3)                 Lengthening

(4)   Pal. Diph.                     Loss-$N$

(5)                 $I$-Mutation

(6)   $U$-Mutation                 Infl.-$W$

(7)   $W$-Infl.       Mut. Pal.          Loss-$G$, -$H$

(8)               Palatal Monophthongisation

**116. General Statements.** It may be well to premise, in order to avoid reiteration,

(1) that EWS. *ie* (*i*), *īe* (*ī*), are invariably replaced in LWS. by *i* and *ī*, or *y* and *ȳ*, usually the latter.

(2) that *eo* and *io* often replace each other in WS., and likewise *ēo* and *īo*, but that WS. *usually prefers* eo *and* ēo, even where *io* and *īo* are etymologically correct. But in the following sections these diphthongs are used *correctly*, i.e.

$$eo < e,\ \bar{e}o < \bar{e},\ io < i,\ \bar{i}o < \bar{i}.$$

(3) that WS. represents the sound of *ǫ* (open *o*), for which it had no distinct sign, by *a* or by *o*, but in this book the sign *ǫ* is used uniformly.

## MUTATION.

**117. Mutation** may be **defined** as the influence exerted upon a stressed vowel by the vowel of a following (usually the next) syllable in the same word, or rarely by a consonant (Mut. Pal.) immediately following, by which influence the vowel-sound of the stressed syllable is modified in anticipation of, and therefore in the direction of, the following ·sound. It is therefore a process of the economy of speech. The vocal organs, for example, eased the effort of transition from a guttural to a palatal vowel by partially palatalising the guttural vowel, as in $\bar{a} > \bar{æ}$.

There are three kinds of mutation in OE.: (1 umbaut.

I. *I-* or *J-*Mutation, called briefly *I-*Mutation or simply Mutation, which was caused by a following *i* or *j* in the same word.

II. *U-* or *O-*Mutation, called briefly *U-*Mutation, which was caused by a following *u* or *o* in the same word.

III. Palatal Mutation, which was caused by a palatal consonant immediately following.

# I. *I*-Mutation.

**118.** *I*-Mutation is the influence exerted by a following *i* or *j* upon the vowel-sound of a stressed syllable, by which that sound is partially assimilated to the sound of the mutating letter. In this mutation, the mutating sounds being palatal, the effect is a palatalisation, i.e. the replacement of a less palatal vowel by a more palatal vowel in every instance. The *i* or *j* that caused the mutation has either disappeared or weakened to *e* in most cases in historic OE.; exceptions, however, are seen in such verbs as *nęrian = nęrjan* (§ 85), and in some adjs., e.g. *hefig* (heavy), *wielisc* (foreign); while numerous traces of mutating *i* and *j* have been pointed out in the Accidence. On the other hand, the *i* in verbs of the 3rd weak class ("Look"), *lōcian*, *lufian*, is a weakening of *ō*, and therefore does not cause *i*-mutation (see § 91).

**Mutation and Gradation.** Mutation is a perfectly simple phenomenon; but the subject has been obscured and confused by its being classed and explained side by side with Gradation, with which it has no conceivable connection except by way of contrast. **Gradation** is a *relation* of *different* vowels in words derived from one root existing side by side *at the same time*; **Mutation** is a *change* of vowel in *one and the same word*, which at one period, therefore, had one vowel-sound, and *at a later time* another (the mutated vowel). Gradation is a *relation* of *different vowels* to one another; Mutation is a *change* in the history of *one vowel*.

**119. Mutation explained.** Great confusion has resulted from loose ideas and statements as to the epoch when derivative words were formed. This is an important point and must be cleared up once for all. From the OE. noun *gold*, it is said, was formed an adjective *gylden*, thus: *gold + in > gylden*. Unfortunately, the OE. *i*-mutation of *o* is *ę*, and if therefore the above adjective had been an OE. formation at all, it would have been *gęlden*, not *gylden*. Again, from an OE. noun *\*wunsc* was formed, it is said, a verb *wȳscan* (wish), thus: *wunsc + ian > wunscian > wūscian > wȳscan*; but, unfortunately, the OE.

noun *wunsc never existed, in all probability. Even Sievers allows himself to speak of the *i*-mutation of *eo* and *ēo*, although he himself states quite clearly elsewhere "that the *e* of the Indo European Parent Speech was regularly changed to Germanic *i* when the next syllable contained an *i* or *j*[1]," that is to say, *in every word, in which OE. i-mutation could possibly take place*. Germanic *e* and *eu* > *i* and *iu*, which in the pre-mutation period of OE. > *io* and *īo* (and *not*, accurately speaking, *eo* and *ēo*).

The truth is simply this: most OE. derivative words are not OE. formations at all, as we know from their existing in one or more of the cognate languages and therefore also in the parent Germanic. Many of them are of immemorial antiquity. This is just as true of the 2nd and 3rd sing. pres. of verbs as of the principal parts. From the remote ancestor of *hātan*, e.g., there had once been formed a 3rd sing. pres. something like *hāteti*. Once formed, this word had an independent existence and came under sound-laws which did not affect *hātan*. It reached the OE. pre-mutation period in the form *hātið* > OE. *hætt*. So with the other words named above. *Gylden* and the OHG. *guldīn* prove the existence of a Germanic parent adjective, whose *i* preserved the radical *u* from change to *o* (§ 98, N. 2) until the OE. *i*-mutation period. OE. *wȳscan* and OHG. *wunsken* prove the existence of a Germanic *wunskjan*, from which of course *wȳscan* is directly descended, and not from an OE. *wunsc, the fictitious parent of a verb with real blue Germanic blood in its veins.

**120.** We have already seen that there was what may be called a Germanic *i*-mutation (§ 98, N. 1, 5), by which *e* > *i* and *eu* > *iu*. There is therefore no OE. mutation *e* > *i*; every such change, as in *hilp(e)ð*, 3rd sing. of *helpan*, *bir(e)ð* of *beran*, *tritt* of *tredan*, in *biddan* and the other "weak presents" of the "Tread" class (cp. pp. *gebeden*), had already occurred in Germanic. But this Germanic *i* could and did, in some words, suffer "breaking" to *io*, and then underwent in OE. a second *i*-mutation, viz. *io* > *ie*.

---

[1] Sievers' *OE. Grammar*, Cook's translation. § 45.

An example is seen in Germanic *herdjo* > *hirdjo* > OE. \**hiordjo* > *hierde*, herdsman. Similarly *eu* underwent double mutation, first in Germanic, then in OE.: *eu* > *iu* > OE. *īo* > *īe*.

*I*-Mutation in OE. can follow Breaking, Pal. Diph., Infl.-*N*, Loss-*N*, and Contraction, and can itself be followed by Infl.-*W*, and Loss-*G*-*H*. Mutated forms of English proper names, such as *Kent*, *Temes*, prove that *I*-Mutation is to be dated after the Saxon Conquest. Pogatscher suggests about the year 600 A.D.

The results of *I*-Mutation in OE. may conveniently be shown as follows:

| | | | | | |
|---|---|---|---|---|---|
| (i) | (a >) æ | > ę (æ) | (ii) | | ā > ǣ |
| (iii) | ea | > ie ⎫ | (iv) | | ēa > īe |
| (v) | io | > ie ⎭ | (vi) | (iu >) | īo > īe |
| (vii) | ǫ, o > ę | | (viii) | | ō > ē |
| (ix) | u | > y | (x) | | ū > ȳ |

**121.** (i) (a >) æ > ę. In positions in which original *a* could suffer *I*-Mutation, it had already become *æ* or *ǫ* (§§ 100 (*b*), 148) before the *I*-Mutation period (except as stated in Note 2).

Examples: *lęgan* (lay), cp. *læg*, past sing. of *licgan*; *sęttan* (set), cp. *sæt*, past sing. of *sittan*; *tęllan*, cp. *talu* (tale); *nęrian* (to save); *męte* (meat), an *i*-stem; *hęll*, a *j*-stem; and "weak presents" of the "Fare" class: *hębban* (raise), cp. pp. *gehafen*; *scęððan* (injure), and *swęrian* (swear).

NOTES. (1) *æ* instead of *ę* is regularly found in the 2nd and 3rd sing. pres. of strong verbs of Class VI.: *færst*, *færð*, from *faran*; in the mutated past parts. of the same Class, *gefæren* ∞ *gefaren*, etc.; in *hæfst*, *hæfð*, from *habban*; in *sægst*, *sægð* ∞ *sęgst*, *sęgð*, from *sęcgan*; in *stæppan* ∞ *stęppan*; and uniformly in *fæstan* (secure), *hæftan* (imprison), etc.

(2) The influence of the *i* (but not *j*) of a final syllable penetrated to the initial syllable and caused mutation, if the second syllable was short and had a guttural vowel. Exs.

aðele (< *aðuli), noble ; gædeling (< *gaduling), relative ; tō-gædere (< *gaduri), together.

**122.** (ii) **ā > ǣ.** Exs.: lǣdan (lead), cp. lād, past of līðan (go) ; lǣfan (leave), cp. lāf, past of līfan (remain) ; lǣran (teach), cp. lār (teaching) ; blǣwð, 3rd sing. of blāwan (blow) ; dǣl (part), an *i*-stem ; lǣwan (betray).

NOTE. OE. (WS.) ǣ, the normal equivalent of Germanic ǣ (W. Germ. ā), is not subject to *i*-mutation. Hence it is not obvious that dǣd, deed, is an *i*-stem, and that lǣce, leech, and mǣre, great, are *j*-stems.

**123.** (iii) **ea > i(e).** Examples: hi(e)lt, wiexð, 3rd sing. pres. of healdan (hold), weaxan (grow) ; slihst, 2nd sing. pres. of slēan (strike) ; mi(e)ht (might), slieht (blow), *i*-stems ; bi(e)ldu (boldness), *i*-stem, cp. beald (bold) : i(e)ldra, compar. of eald (old) ; hli(e)hhan (laugh) ; cwielman (torment), cp. cwealm (destruction) ; giest (guest), *i*-stem ; sci(e)ppan (create), " weak-present."

NOTE. EWS. i(e), ī(e), whatever their origin, are regularly replaced later by y, ȳ, which sometimes appear in EWS. For i(e) < ea EWS. not infrequently has y before l or r : yldest ∝ ieldest (oldest) ; gewyldan ∝ gewi(e)ldan (control) ; dyrne ∝ dierne (secret) ; wyrnan ∝ wiernan (refuse).

**124.** (iv) **ēa > ī(e).** Examples: hīewð, hlīepð, 3rd sing. pres. of the Reduplicating verbs, hēawan (hew), hlēapan (leap) ; līeg (flame), *i*-stem ; nīeten (small animal), cp. nēat (animal) ; hīehst, superl. of hēah (high) ; ālī(e)fan (allow) ; gelī(e)fan (believe) ; cīese (cheese).

**125.** (v) **io > i(e).** Here belong all the examples usually given under *eo*, as explained in § 119: fi(e)ht, wi(e)rð, 3rd sing. pres. of feohtan (fight), weorðan (become) ; gesi(e)hð, gefi(e)hð, 3rd sing. pres. of gesēon (see), gefēon (rejoice) ; hi(e)rde (herdsman), cp. heord (herd) ; bi(e)rhtu (brightness), cp. beorht (bright) ; fierst (time), *i*-stem ; wi(e)rðe (worthy), cp. weorð (worth) ; āfierran (remove), cp. feorr (far) ; liehtan (make easy), cp. lioht (light, easy).

**126.** (vi) īo > īe, ī. Here belong all the examples usually given under īo, as explained in § 119: crīepþ, scīet, 3rd sing. pres. of crēopan (creep), scēotan (shoot); getrīewe (true), cp. trēow (truth); līe(e)htan (illuminate), cp. lēoht (light); stī(e)ran (guide), cp. stēor (guidance); strīenan (obtain), cp. gestrēon (possessions); as well as frīend, frīend, dat. sing. and nom. pl. of fīond (enemy), frīond (friend).

**127.** (vii) ǫ, o > ę. (a) Examples of ǫ > ę: stęnt, 3rd sing. pres. of stǫndan (stand); bęnd (bond), i-stem, cp. bǫnd, past sing. of bindan; męn(n), dat. and pl. of mǫn(n), man; stręngra, compar. of strǫng; fręmman (perform), cp. frǫm (bold); nęmnan (to name), cp. nǫma (name); sęndan (to send), cp. sǫnd (message); tęmian (to tame), cp. tǫm (tame).

(b) The only examples of o > ę are: dęhter, dat. of dohtor (daughter); ęxen, pl. of oxa (ox); męrgen (morn), cp. morgen; ęfes (eaves); ęle (oil).

**128.** (viii) ō > ē. Exs.: blēwþ, grēwþ, 3rd sing. pres. of the Reduplicating verbs blōwan (bloom), grōwan; the "weak-present" wēpan (weep), cp. pp. wōpen; swēg (sound), cp. swōgan (to roar); brēðer, dat. of brōðor; swēte (sweet), cp. swōte (sweetly); dēman (to judge), cp. dōm (doom); ēfstan (to hasten), cp. ōfost (haste); sēcan (to seek), cp. sōhte (sought); cwēn (woman), i-stem; gecwēman (to please); gēs, dat. and pl. of gōs (goose); smēðe (smooth), cp. smōðe (smoothly); gesīðan (to prove), cp. sōð (true); ēhtan (to pursue), cp. ōht (persecution); fēhst, fēhð, 2nd and 3rd sing. pres. of fōn (to seize).

**129.** (ix) u > y. Exs.: cymþ, 3rd sing. pres. of cuman (come); the "past-present" subjunctives dyge, dyrre, gemyne, scyle, ðyrfe, cp. dugon, etc.; hyngran (to hunger), cp. hungor; gesynto (health), cp. gesund (sound); byr(i)g, dat. of burg (fort); pytt (pit); wylfen (she-wolf), cp. wulf; wyllen (woollen), cp. wull; fyllan (fill), cp. full. In nearly all other instances, such as gylden (golden), gyden (goddess), bycgan (buy), y appears to be the i-mutation of o (in gold, god, bohte), as it is still often said to be.

But the truth is that y cannot possibly be the mutation of o; for not only is ę the mutation of o, and no vowel has two mutated forms; but we have already seen that Germanic u was protected by a following i, j, from the change into o, which was undergone by the pair-words *gold, god, bohte*, etc. (see § 98, N. 2).

NOTE. After palatal g, c, sc, we not infrequently find i for y: *gingra, gingest* (always with i), compar. and superl. of *iung, geong* (young); *scile* ∞ *scyle*, etc.

**130.** (x) ū > ȳ. Examples: *brȳcð, lȳcð*, 3rd sing. pres. of *brūcan* (enjoy), *lūcan* (lock); *brȳd* (bride), *fȳst* (fist), *i*-stems; *cȳðan* (to make known), cp. *cūð* (known); *fȳsan* (to hasten), cp. *fūs* (eager); *wȳscan* (to wish).

## II. U-MUTATION.

**131.** *U*-Mutation (under which we include *O*-Mutation) is the influence exercised by a following guttural vowel upon a stressed i, e, or a, in consequence of which, i.e. in anticipation of the following guttural vowel, a guttural glide-sound arose after the stressed vowel, and in time formed a diphthong with it. Thus

(i)    i + a, o, u > io,
(ii)   e + a, o, u > eo,
(iii) a +        u > ea (= æa).

The vowel a does not suffer o-mutation in WS., and u-mutation of a is very rare. Indeed the effects of this influence generally are very limited in WS., as compared with the other dialects. The guttural vowels that caused this mutation, being vowels of unstressed syllables, have so frequently weakened in historic times, u to o, o to a, etc., that some knowledge of prehistoric forms is necessary in order to discriminate u-mutations from o (a)-mutations.

U-Mutation could be followed, in the history of the same word, by W-Infl. (§ 114), but no other change either preceded or followed it. It is uniformly wanting before *c* and *g*. In most words in which this mutation is seen, forms with the original vowel unchanged are also found.

**132.** (i) i > io (eo). This is by far the most extensive of the three effects in WS. It is especially common in EWS. Later, the sound reverted to simple *i*, or the effect was disguised by the operation of W-Infl. Examples are:

(*a*) *u*-mutations:

freoðo, *peace*            siolofr, seolfor, *silver*
mioloc, meolc, *milk*      liomu, *pl. of* lim, *limb*
siodu, *custom*            swiotul, sweotol, *clear*

(*b*) *o(a)*-mutations:

wiotan, *counsellors*      cliopian, *to call*
hiora, *of them*           tiolian, *to aim at*
nioðor, *downwards*        liofað, *lives* (from *libban*)
neoðan, *from beneath*

NOTE. It is to be remembered that most of the above words are also found in EWS. with original *i* unchanged: *hira*, *sido*, etc.

**133.** (ii) e > eo is pretty common, but is not as a rule caused by inflectional *u*. Examples are:

(*a*) *u*-mutations:

eofor, *boar*              weorod, *troop*
heofon, *heaven*           sweostor, *sister*
heorot, *hart*             seofon, *seven*.

(*b*) *o(a)*-mutations:

weola, *weal*              weorold, *world*

**134.** (iii) a > ea is very rare in EWS. prose, being found only in the three words *ealu*, gen. *ealoð* (ale), *cearu* (sorrow), *sleacnes* (slackness). As forms with *ea* are common in poetical texts, it is probable that they adopted the *ea* from the Anglian originals: *beadu*, *heaðu-*, battle; *cafoð*, strength, etc.

Notes. (1) The *ea* in *bearu* (grove), *bealu* (evil), etc., is a "breaking" borrowed from the oblique cases, *bearwes* (§ 136), etc. On the other hand, the *ea* of *geatu*, pl. of *geat* (gate), is borrowed from the sing. (§§ 100, 143).

(2) The *protecting* influence of a following guttural vowel we have already seen in the retention of original *a*, *ā*, in *dagas*, *fatu*, *magas*, etc. (§§ 100, 105).

## III. PALATAL MUTATION.

**135.** Palatal Mutation is the palatalisation of a stressed vowel through the influence of a palatal consonant immediately following. It is of little importance in WS. in comparison with the other dialects. There are four cases, one of which is doubtful, and two more of which are confined to LWS. In three of the four cases Palatal Mutation follows Breaking: no other change either preceded or followed it. The four cases are as follows:

(i) *eo* > *i(e)* in EWS. in the four words *cni(e)ht*, servant, *riht*[1], right, *wri(e)xl*, exchange, and *si(e)x*, six. In these words, guttural *h* (x = hs), which had 'broken' *e* to *eo*, became palatal and then palatalised the preceding vowel. In *feohtan*, *gefeoht* (fight), there was no further change.

(ii) *ea* > *i(e)* in *ni(e)ht* (night) in EWS., and later in *mihte* < *meahte* (could) and *mihtig* (mighty). This is the doubtful case; but it is difficult to see to what other cause than Palatal Mutation the change can be attributed.

Note. *Mi(e)ht* (might) is an *i*-stem and its change of vowel is therefore an *i*-mutation; but *ni(e)ht* (night) belongs to a class (§ 39) of nouns which suffer *i*-mutation in the oblique sing. and nom. pl. only.

[1] *Riht* occurs but three times in EWS.; elsewhere always *ryht*.

(iii) ea > e **in LWS.** before *h* (*x*). Examples: *seh* < *seah* (saw); *sleh* < *sleah*, 2nd sing. imperative of *slēan* (strike).

(iv) ēa > ē **in LWS.** before *h, g, c*. Examples are seen in the past sing. of strong verbs of Class II.: *tēh* < *tēah* from *tēon*, to draw; *bēg* < *bēag* from *būgan*, to bow; *lēc* < *lēac* from *lūcan*, to lock; and in *ðēh* < *ðēah* (though), etc. This is the case in which Breaking did not precede.

## IV. BREAKING.

**136.** Breaking is a process of the same nature as *U*-Mutation, but was caused by following guttural *consonants*. To ease the transition from the palatal vowels æ (< *a*), *e*, *i*, to a guttural *h*, covered *l* (i.e. *l* followed by another consonant), or covered *r*, immediately following, a guttural glide-sound arose, which soon formed a diphthong with the preceding vowel. Thus

(i) (a >) **æ + u** + *h*, *r* (+ const.), *l* (+ const.) > **ea** + etc.

(ii) **e + o** + *h*, *r* (+ const.), *l* (+ *c* or *h*) > **eo** + etc.

(iii) **i + o** + *h*, *r* (+ const.), > **io** (eo) + etc.

This table shows at a glance the vowels affected by breaking, its causes and conditions, and its results. Although the vowels affected and the results are the same as in the similar process of *U*-Mutation, it is only rarely possible to confound the two. Except in monosyllables, where *u*-mutation is necessarily impossible, breaking was always conditioned by two following consonants; whereas *u*-mutation did not penetrate through two consonants, except in rare instances (such as *sweostor*, *ðiossum* = *ðissum*).

Breaking follows Shortening (of *ī*); it can be followed, in the history of one and the same word, by *I*-Mutation, Palatal Mutation, Pal. Mon., *W*-Infl., and Loss-*H*.

**137.** (i) (a >) æ > **ea** before *h* (*x*), covered *r*, and covered *l*. Examples are numerous: *feallan* (fall), *healdan* (hold), *weaxan* (grow), of the Reduplicating class of strong verbs; past sing. of strong verbs of the "Help" class: *healp* from *helpan*, *wearð* from *weorðan* (to become), *feaht* from *feohtan* (to fight); hence in the "past-present" verbs *dear(r)*, *ðearf*, of the 3rd strong class; *seah* from *sēon* (see); similarly in the "past-present" verb *be-, ge-neah* (it suffices); *sleah*, sing. imperat. of *slēan* (strike); *meaht, meahte*, parts of the "past-present" verb *mæg*; *feax* (hair); *Wealh* (Welshman); *Seaxan* (Saxons); *cealc* (chalk), a foreign word introduced at an early period; all the forms of *bearu* (grove), *bealu* (evil), *searu* (armour), and of the adjs. *gearu* (yare), *nearu* (narrow), in the uninflected forms of all which the broken vowel is borrowed from the oblique cases; *eald* (old); *eall* (all); *earm* (wretched); *eahta* (eight); *earnian* (to earn).

NOTES. (1) *a* before covered *l* sometimes remains: *fallan, haldan, ald, all, Walh*.

(2) *ll* < earlier *l + j* does not cause breaking, because the *ll* had become palatal: *hell* (hell), *j*-stem; *sellan* (give); *tellan* (tell).

(3) Metathesis of *r* took place after the Breaking-period; hence there is no breaking in *berst* (burst), *bærnan* (burn, trans.), *ærn* (house), *gærs* (grass), nor in *berstan* (burst), *ðerscan* (thresh); but, exceptionally, *beornan* < *brinnan* (burn, intrans.) has a broken vowel.

**138.** (ii) e > **eo** before *h*, covered *r*, *lc* and *lh*. Examples: *feohtan* (fight), *weorpan* (throw), of the "Help" class; *seoh*, sing. imperat. of *sēon*; *cneoht* (a servant); *eorðe* (earth); *heord* (herd); *seolh* (seal), cp. *helm* (helmet); *steorra* (star); *seolf* (self), exceptional form of *self*; *teohhian* (arrange); *meolcan* (milk).

**139.** (iii) i > **io** (eo) before *h* and covered *r*; but examples are few, because in many words *i*-mutation supervened (see § 125): *Wioht* (Isle of Wight), *beornan* (to burn), *leornian* (to learn), *leoht* (light, easy), *betweoh, betweox* (betwixt).

## V. GLIDE-DIPHTHONGISATION[1].

**140.** The above name is used here to denote a process, similar in character to *U*-Mutation and Breaking, and perhaps arising in imitation of them, but differing from them in that the 'glide' is palatal. It is probable that, in imitation of *i* > *io* before guttural *r*, *i* > *ie* before a palatalised *r*, and then the same diphthongisation arose before other consonants. It follows, and is followed by, no other change. In every word in which it is seen, unchanged *i* is also found. Examples are: *bi(e)rnan* (burn), *iernan* (run), of the "Drink" class; *bi(e)rst*, *bi(e)rð*, 2nd and 3rd sing. of *beran* (bear); *bi(e)rst*, 2nd and 3rd sing. of *berstan* (burst); *hi(e)re*, gen. and dat. of *hēo* (she); *hi(e)ne*, acc. of *hē* (he); *gi(e)fð*, *ongi(e)tt* (§ 120), 3rd sing. of *giefan*, *ongietan* (§ 77); *si(e)ndon* (are).

## VI. PALATAL DIPHTHONGISATION.

**141.** The above name is given to a series of changes which consist in the introduction of a palatal 'glide' (i *or* e) between an initial palatal consonant (j, g, sc, c) and a following stressed vowel; the 'glide' afterwards formed a diphthong with the following vowel, and then, being the first element of the diphthong, took over the stress. This is the general nature of the change; the particular cases are somewhat numerous, occurring, as they do, in the downward history of Germanic stressed *e, a, o, u, ā, ō, ū, ai*. They are conveniently summarised in three classes:

(i) Palatalisation of *ǣ, o, ō, u, ū* after initial *j*.

(ii) Palatalisation of primary[2] *e, æ, ǣ* after initial palatalised *c, g, sc*.

(iii) Palatalisation of *a, ā, o, ę, ō, u, ū*, after initial palatalised *sc*.

---

[1] This name is equally applicable to *U*-Mutation and Breaking; but they are already better named; and a similar objection might be urged against the term Mutation, which could of course be used of any change whatever.

[2] I.e. the *normal* OE. developments of Germanic *e, a, ǣ*.

Palatal Diphthongisation could follow Infl.-N and Lengthening; and could itself be followed by I-Mutation (as in *scieppan*, create; *cīese*, cheese), by Loss-G (*ongēan*, against), and by Pal. Mon. (see § 145).

Notes. (1) Breaking is prior to Pal. Diph. and has the preference. Hence *cerfan (carve) > ceorfan, not cierfan. Hence also the *ea* in *geald* is a 'breaking,' whereas the infin. of the same verb, *gieldan* (pay), shows Pal. Diph.

(2) A following *u* or *o* prevents Pal. Diph., and preserves the stressed vowel for subsequent *u*-mutation: e.g. *gelo (yellow) > geolo, not gielo. The *ie* of *giefu* (gift) is due to analogy with the oblique *giefe*, and the *ea* of *geatu* (gates) to analogy with the singular *geat*.

**142.** (i) **After initial j**[1] the following changes occurred—examples are scarce, because but few OE. words began with *j*:

(a) $\bar{a}$ > $\bar{\imath}a$ in *gēa*, yea; *gēar*, year.

(b) *o* > *eo(io)* in *geoc*, yoke.

(c) $\bar{o}$ (< $\bar{a}$ by Infl.-N.) > $\bar{e}o$ in *gēomor*, sad.

(d) *u*, $\bar{u}$, sometimes remain, as in *iung*, young, *iuguð*, youth, *iū* (< *ju*), formerly;

but usually > *eo(io)*, $\bar{e}o$, as in *geong*, *geoguð*, *gēo*.

**143.** (ii) **After initial palatalised c, g, sc, primary e, æ, ǣ** regularly suffered the following changes in EWS.:

(a) **e > ie.** Examples: *gieldan* (pay), *giellan* (yell), of Class "Help"; *scieran* (cut), of Class "Bear"; *giefan* (give), *ongietan* (perceive), pp. *ongieten*, of Class "Tread."

Note. (1) Forms with *i* are also found: *gildan*, *gifan*, etc.

(b) (a >) **æ > ea.** Examples: *scear*, past sing. of *scieran*; *geaf, -geat*, past sing. of *giefan, -gietan*; the "past-present" verb *sceal* (shall); *ceaster* (fort), *geat* (gate), etc. In *giest* (stranger), *scieppan* (create), < *geasti, *sceappjan, Pal. Diph. has been followed by I-Mutation.

---

[1] There is no character *j* in OE.; the symbols *i* and *g* were used, usually the latter, as in the above examples. It is only by knowing the history of a word that *g* (=*j*) can be distinguished from *g* (=*g*).

(c) **ǣ > ēa.** Examples: *scēaron*, past pl. of *scieran*; *gēafon*, *-gēaton*, past pl. of *giefan*, *-gietan*; *scēap* (sheep). In *cīese < \*cēasi*, Pal. Diph. has been followed by *I*-Mutation.

NOTE. (2) Only primary *e*, *æ*, *ǣ*, suffer this change. The mutated vowels *ę*, *ǣ*, *ǣ* (§§ 121, 122, 127) are unaffected by it: *gescępen* (pp. of *scieppan*), *gædeling*, *tǣgædere*.

**144.** (iii) **After initial sc, guttural vowels** suffered the following changes, but *not uniformly*; in every word in which the changes are seen, the original vowel is also found, even in the same text.

(*a*) *a > ea*, seen in verbs of the "Fare" class, e.g. *sceacan ∞ scacan* (shake), pp. *sc(e)acen*.

(*b*) *ā > ēa*, seen in *scēadan ∞ scādan* (to distinguish) of the Reduplicating class.

(*c*) *o > eo*, seen in *sceop ∞ scop* (bard), *sceolde ∞ scolde* from *sceal* (shall).

(*d*) *ǫ > eo*, seen in *sceomu ∞ scǫmu* (shame).

(*e*) *ō > ēo*, seen in past tenses of the "Fare" class, e.g. *scēoc ∞ scōc* (shook), *scēop ∞ scōp* from *scieppan*.

(*f*) *u > eo*, seen in *sceolon ∞ sculon*, pl. of the "past-present" verb *sceal* (shall). This *eo* may be borrowed from *sceolde* above, since it is the only instance in EWS.

(*g*) *ū > ēo* in **LWS.** only: *scēofan ∞ scūfan* (shove).

## VII. PALATAL MONOPHTHONGISATION.

**145.** This is a process which consists in the change of the diphthongs *ea*, *ēa*, into the palatal monophthongs *e*, *ē*, through the influence of initial palatal *j*, *c*, *g*, *sc*. It is frequently the completion of the palatalising process begun in Pal. Diph., but it may also follow Breaking and Loss-*G*. It is itself followed by no other change. It is seen in the downward history of Germanic *a*, *ǣ* and *au*.

NOTE. Sievers makes the tactical error of including this phenomenon under Palatal Mutation, although, being a *forward* influence, it is excluded by his definition of Mutation.

Classified examples are:

(a) Following on Pal. Diph.:—*gef* < *geaf* (gave), *onyet* < *ongeat* (perceived), *scel* < *sceal* (shall), *cester* < *ceaster* (castle); *ongēten* < *ongēaten*, past subjunctive of *ongietan*. After *j*:—*yēr* < *yēar*.

(b) Following on Breaking:—*celf* < *cealf* (calf).

(c) Following on Loss-*G*:—*ongēn* (against) < *ongēan* < *onyeagn* (Pal. Diph.).

(d) **In LWS.** *ēa* (< Germ. *au*) > *ē*, as in the past sing. of verbs of the "Creep" class: *cēs* < *cēas* (chose), *gēt* < *gēat* (poured), *scēt* < *scēat* (shot).

## VIII. INFLUENCE OF PRECEDING *W*.

**146.** The semi-vowel *w* has a close affinity to the vowels *u* and *o*, and its influence tends to substitute one of them for the diphthongs *io*, *eo*, arisen through Breaking or *U*-Mutation. This change therefore in almost every instance follows Breaking or *U*-Mutation; it is itself followed by no other change.

The two chief cases, with selected examples, are:

(a) **wio** usually > **wu** (and even *u*), but both *wi* and *wio* sometimes remain:—*wudu* (wood), rarely *wiodu*; *wuduwe* (widow), beside *widuwe*; *wuht* (wight, thing), beside *wiht*; *swutol* (clear), beside *swiotol*; *bet(w)uh*, *bet(w)ux* (betwixt), beside *betwih*, *betweoh*, etc.

(b) *weo* usually remained, but also > *wo* and in LWS. *wu*:—*worold* (world) < *weorold*; *worðig* (street) < *weorðig*; *swustor* (sister), LWS. *swustor*, < *sweostor*; LWS. *swurd* (sword) < *sweord*.

NOTE. Apparently isolated instances of *wo* < *wa* are seen in *gesworen*, pp. of *swęrian* (§ 80), and *geðwogen*, pp. of *ðwēan* (§ 78).

## IX. INFLUENCE OF FOLLOWING W.

**147.** To ease the transition between *a*, *e*, *ę*, and following *w*, a *u-*'glide' arose, which with the preceding vowels formed the diphthongs *au*, *eu*, and these normally passed into EWS. *ēa*, *ēo* (§§ 111, 112). The only other change with which this came into relation was *I*-Mutation, by which it was preceded in several words. In all, however, there are but few examples.

(*a*) *aw > auw > ēaw*, seen in *fēaw*, few.

(*b*) *ew > euw > ēow*, seen in the inflected forms of *ðēo(w)*, servant, *cnēo(w)*, knee, *trēo(w)*, tree, e.g. gen. sg. *ðēowes*, *cnēowes*.

NOTES. (1) The *ēo* of the nom. sg. is due to vocalisation of the *w* and contraction, *w* being afterwards borrowed from the oblique cases.

(2) *Gesewen*, pp. of *sēon* (see), is an exception.

(*c*) Following *I*-Mutation, *ęw > euw > ēow*, seen in *mēowle* (maid), *strēowede ∝ strewede* (strewed), etc.

## X. INFLUENCE OF FOLLOWING NASAL.

**148.** The influence of a following nasal, already seen in Germanic (§ 98, N. 1, 2), produced in the prehistoric OE. period the five following well marked changes:

|        | Germ. |   | OE. |
|--------|-------|---|-----|
| (i)    | a     | > | ǫ   |
| (ii)   | e     | > | i   |
| —(iii) | o     | > | u   |
| (iv)   | ǣ     | > | ō̧  |
| (v)    | ā     | > | ō   |

This is one of the earliest of the OE. influences, being perhaps synchronous with Breaking. It can be followed by Pal. Diph., Loss-*N*, and *I*-Mutation, and even by the last two in succession in the same word (e.g. *gēs*).

**149.** (i) a > ǫ. Examples:—*mǫn(n)*, man; *lǫnd*, land; *lǫng*, long; and the "past-present" verbs, *ǫn(n)*, grant; *cǫn(n)*, know (how to); *(ge)mǫn*, remember.

NOTES. (1) OE. had no distinctive symbol for the sound of open o, and therefore used both *a* and *o* to denote this sound, more often *o* in EWS. This very fluctuation of symbol points to a sound different from both *a* and *o*. It must not be supposed that the sound varied with the symbol, which often fluctuated in the same text.

(2) In a few weak-stressed words, such as *on*, in; the masc. accus. *ðone*, *hwone*, the neuter instr. *ðon*, *hwon*, from *sē*, *hwā*; the advs. *ðonne*, then, *hwonne*, when, etc., *o* is almost invariably found, and we may therefore conclude that the sound was *o*, not ǫ.

**150.** (ii) e > i, seen in *niman*, take; and in early borrowings from Latin, e.g. *gim(m)*, gem; *pinsian*, consider.

NOTES. (1) Examples are few, chiefly because *e* > *i* in Germanic before nasal plus consonant (§ 98, N. 1); partly because of the exceptions, *cwene*, woman, *denu*, valley, and the late or "learned" borrowing *temp(e)l*, temple.

(2) The history of *cuman* (to come) is probably this: \**cweman* > \**cwiman* (Infl.-N) > \**cwuman* (W-Infl.) > *cuman*.

**151.** (iii) o > u. Exs.: *(ge)cumen*, *genumen*, pps. of *cuman*, come, *niman*, take; *wunian*, dwell; and the early borrowings from Latin: *munuc*, monk; *nunne*, nun; *munt*, mount; *pund*, pound; etc. Not in *font*, font, which is therefore probably late.

**152.** (iv) Germ. ǣ > W. Germ. ā > OE. ō. Exs.:— *c(w)ōmon*, *nōmon*, past pls. of *cuman*, *niman*; *gedōn*, pp. of *dōn*, do; *mōna*, moon; *mōnað*, month; *sōna*, soon; etc.

(v) (W.) Germ. ā̃ (§ 98, N. 3) > OE. ō. Exs.:—

fōn, *seize*      brōhte, *brought*     ōht, *persecution*
hōn, *hang* (§ 81)    ðōhte, *thought* (§ 90)   wōh, *crooked*

NOTE. It may be wondered how this last change comes under Infl.-N. The very fact that this *ā* underwent the same change to *ō* as the *ā* in (iv) above, proves that this *ā* had a certain nasal quality surviving from the following *n* lost in the Germanic period, which justifies its classification under Nasal Influence.

## XI. COMPENSATORY LENGTHENING FOR LOSS OF NASAL.

**153.** Just as in Germanic every $a$, $i$, $u$, occurring before $nh$, $> \bar{a}$, $\bar{i}$, $\bar{u}$ in compensation for the loss of the $n$; so in the prehistoric OE. period, ($a >$) $ǫ > \bar{o}$, $i > \bar{i}$, and $u > \bar{u}$ in compensation for the loss of $n$ or $m$ before the three other voiceless spirants, $f$, $s$, $ð$. This change may be preceded by Infl.-$N$ (in the change $a > ǫ$), and is frequently followed by $I$-Mutation (§§ 128, 130).

Classified examples are :

(a) $i > \bar{i}$ :—$sīð$, journey ; $strīð$, strong ; $fīf$ ($< fimf$), five.

(b) $ǫ > \bar{o}$ :—$gōs$, goose ; $tōð$, tooth ; $ōðer$, second ; $sōð$, true ; $smōðe$, smoothly ; $sōfte$ ($< sǫmfte$), softly.

(c) $u > \bar{u}$ :—$hūsl$, 'housel'; $mūð$, mouth ; $ūs$, us ; $cūðe$, $cūð$, $ūðe$, parts of the "past-present" verbs $cunnan$ (know), $unnan$ (grant).

NOTE. $N$ is lost in all the above words but $fīf$ and $sōfte$.

## XII. CONTRACTION.

**154.** Contraction is the blending of two following vowel-sounds into one in order to avoid hiatus. The two sounds have in most instances been brought together through the loss of a consonant, usually $h$, sometimes $j$ or $w$, rarely another consonant ; but there are many instances in which no consonant has been lost. There are two kinds of Contraction. Contraction proper, in which original $a$, $\bar{a}$, $e$, $i$, or $\bar{i}$ forms **a diphthong** with the following vowel, and which is almost always preceded by the loss of a consonant ; and Absorption, in which a long vowel, OE. $\bar{a}$, $\bar{æ}$, $\bar{o}$, $\bar{u}$, $\bar{y}$, $ēa$, $ēo$, simply absorbs the following unstressed vowel, and which is often not preceded by the loss of a consonant. Contraction proper is rarely followed by $I$-Mutation ; no other change precedes or follows it. Absorption is much later in date, and can follow Breaking and $I$-Mutation.

The following are the most important cases:

(i)  a, ā (+ h, w) + guttural vowel > ēa
(ii) e    (+ h)   +    „        „   > ēo
(iii) i, ī (+ h, j) +   „        „   > īo (ēo)
(iv) i    (+ j)   + e               > ie
(v)  **Absorptions.**

**155.** (i) W. Germ. a, ā + guttural vowel > ēa after loss of *h* or *w*. Examples: the contracted verbs of the "Fare" class: slēan (< *slahan), slay; flēan, flay; lēan, blame; þwēan, wash; and all present forms of the same, except 2nd and 3rd sing. indic. and 2nd sing. imperat.: slēa, (I) slay, etc.; tēar (< *tahur), tear; ēa (< *ah(w)u), water; clēa < clāwu, claw; nēar (< *nāhor), nearer.

**156.** (ii) e + guttural vowel > ēo after loss of *h*. Examples:—the contracted verbs of the "Tread" class: gefēon (< *gefehan), rejoice; plēon, adventure: sēon (< *seh(w)an), see; gefēo, (I) rejoice, etc.; past tenses in ēo of the Reduplicating class, resulting from the contraction of the *e* of the reduplicated syllable with the following stressed vowel: hēold (< *hehald), hēoldon, held; fēold (< *fefald), folded, etc.; twēo (< *tweho), doubt; tēoða (< *tehoða), tenth.

**157.** (iii) i, ī + guttural vowel > īo, ēo after loss of *h* or *j*, or without loss of consonant. Examples:—the contracted verbs of the "Shine" class: ðīon (< *ðihan), thrive; lēon, lend; tēon, accuse; wrīon, cover; ðēo, (I) thrive, etc.; bēot (< *bihāt), boast; betwēonum (< *bitwihunum), between; fīond (< *fijand), enemy; frēond, friend; hīo (< hi- + u), she; sēo, fem. of sē, that.

NOTE. The mutation of this īo (ēo) is seen in the dat. sing. and nom. pl. fīend, frīend.

(iv) i + e > ie after loss of *j*. Examples: sīe (< *sije), be; hīe, her, they; ðrīe, three.

**158. Absorptions.** Selected examples are arranged under the absorbing vowels:

(a) **ā + vowel > ā**:—*tā* (< *tāhe*), toe; *rā*, roe; *gān* (< *gāan*), go.

(b) **ǣ + vowel > ǣ**:—*sǣs* (< \**sǣes*), gen. of *sǣ*, sea; *ǣ* (< \**ǣe*), oblique sing. of *ǣ*, law.

(c) **ō + vowel > ō**:—the contracted verbs of the Reduplicating class: *fōn* (< \**fōhan*), seize; *hōn*, hang; and all present forms of the same, except 2nd and 3rd sing. indic. and 2nd sing. imperat.: *fō*, (I) seize, etc.; *dōn* (< \**dōan*), do; *wōs* (< \**wōhes*), gen. of *wōh*, crooked.

(d) *ū* + vowel sometimes > *ū*:—*gebūn* (< *gebūen*), *gebūd* (< \**gebūed*), pp. of *būan*, *būgean*, dwell.

(e) *ȳ* + vowel sometimes > *ȳ*:—*drȳs* (< \**drȳes*), gen. of *drȳ*, magician; but pl. *drȳas*, etc.

(f) **ēa + vowel > ēa**:—*frēa* (< \**frauja*), lord; several inflected forms of *hēah*, high: *hēas* (< \**hēahes*), etc. (§ 46); its weak form, *hēa*, etc.; *fēa* (< *fēawe*), dat. *fēam*, few.

(g) **ēo + vowel > ēo**:—the contracted verbs of the "Creep" class: *flēon* (< \**fleuhan*), flee; *tēon*, draw; *flēo*, (I) flee; *flēonde*, fleeing, etc.

Notes. (1) It seems better to attribute such forms as *ēos*, gen. of *eoh*, horse, *fēos*, gen. of *feoh*, money, to Compensatory Lengthening for Loss of *h* plus Absorption, than to simple Contraction, i.e. *ēos* < \**ēoes* < \**eohes* rather than *ēos* < \**eo(h)es*; because on the latter supposition Contraction must have followed Breaking, which seems improbable; whereas Absorption is a much later change, as has been stated.

(2) Unstressed *e* is lost in *be* and *ne* in composition with words beginning with a vowel or *w*:—*būtan* < *be-ūtan*, *nān* < *ne ān*, *næs* < *ne wæs*, *nyllað* < *ne willað*.

# XIII. COMPENSATORY LENGTHENING FOR LOSS OF *G* OR *H*.

**159. Loss of h** between vowels is seen in Contraction (and Absorption). *H* is also lost between a resonant (*l*, *m*, *n*, *r*) and a following vowel, with compensatory lengthening of the preceding vowel. This loss is almost always preceded by Breaking or *I*-Mutation; in one instance (ðyrel and its derivatives) it is preceded by both.

Examples are :— *hōles*, gen. of *holh*, hole; *Wēalas*, pl. of *Wealh*, Briton; *mēares*, gen. sg. of *mearh*, horse; *fēore*, dat. sg. of *feorh*, life; *corod* (< \**coh-rād*), troop; *frōlan* (< \**frolhan*), penetrate; *ōret* (< \**or-hāt*), battle; *ðyrel* (< \**ðyrhil* < \**ðurhil*), aperture; *ðwēal* (< \**ðweahl*), bath.

NOTE. In the last example the resonant follows the *h*, and there is no following vowel. Several instances will be found in the Accidence of this disappearance of *h* before a resonant, but after a vowel which is already long: *hēane*, *hēara* from *hēah*, high; *wōne*, *wōra* < *wōhne*, etc., from *wōh*, crooked; *hīera*, higher. The same thing is seen in the compounds *hēalic*, high; *nēalǣcan*, approach. Forms with *h* are probably only etymological spellings.

**160. Loss of g** often took place between a palatal vowel and *n*, *d*, or *ð*, with compensatory lengthening of the vowel; but forms with *g* are also very common. This loss could follow *I*-Mutation or Palatal Diphthongisation.

Examples :— *brēdan*, *brǣd*, *brūdon*, *gebrōden*, < *bregdan*, etc., to shake, of the "Help" class; *frīnan*, *frānon*, *gefrūnen* < *frignan*, etc., to inquire, of the "Drink" class; *sǣde* < *sægde*, past of *secgan*, say; *lēde*, *gelēd*, < *legde*, *gelegd*, from *lecgan*, lay; *mǣden* < *magden*, maiden; *ongēan* (< *ongeagn*), against; *ðēn* < *ðegn*, thane; *līð* < *ligð*, from *licgan*, lie; *tīðian* < *tigðian*, grant; *oferhȳd* < *oferhygd*, arrogance.

NOTE. Four examples after a *guttural* vowel, *u* or *o*, are included above; they are doubtless due to analogy with the other parts of the same verbs.

## XIV. LENGTHENING.

**161.** Lengthening of the final vowel of a monosyllable is common, especially after the loss of a final consonant. Examples:—*swā*, so; *bī*, by; *ðū*, thou; *nū*, now; and after loss of final consonant:—*mē*, (to) me; *wē*, we; *yē*, ye; *hē*, he (all four with $\bar{e} < e < i$); *hwā*, who; and the prefix *ā-* (§ 174).

## XV. SHORTENING.

**162.** Shortening of *ī* to *i*, followed by Breaking, is seen in the adjective *leoht* = *lioht* (< \**liht*), light (not heavy), and in the prep. *betweoh* < *betwih*, betwixt (§ 146).

## C. UPWARD HISTORY: SELECTED EXAMPLES.

**163.** In order to complement the two preceding divisions on the Downward History and the Sound-Laws of the stressed vowels, we start here with the OE. vowel-sounds and give in tabular form the principal stages in their development from the Germanic vowels. Almost every possible 'genealogy' of the OE. vowels is illustrated by one example: on the left is the OE. word; from left to right are given the successive stages through which its stressed vowel has passed; on the right is an example of the original vowel from another Germanic language. The Sound-Laws under which each change comes are indicated by abbreviations (§ 114); when no such indication is given, it is implied that the change is normal (§§ 100—13), or independent. It must be remembered that these are only illustrations: some of them stand for the history of the stressed vowels of many OE. words; in the case of a few, it might be difficult to adduce a single other example. With this caution, the table may be used in a variety of ways.

## Short Vowels.

| OE. | | |
|---|---|---|
| **a** | | |
| faran, *go* | a < a | OHG.[1] faran |
| | | |
| **æ** | | |
| dæg, *day* | æ < a | Go. dags |
| færð, *goes* | æ (Mut.) < æ < a | Go. fariþ |
| | | |
| **e** | | |
| beran, *bear* | e < e | OHG. beran |
| gef, *gave* | e (Pal. Mon.) < ea (Pal. Diph.) < æ < a | Go. gaf |
| celf, *calf* | e (Pal. Mon.) < ea (Brkᵍ) < æ < a | OHG. calb |
| LWS. fex, *hair* | e (Mut. Pal.) < ea (Brkᵍ) < æ < a | OHG. fahs |
| mec, *me* | e < i | OHG. mih |
| | | |
| **ę** | | |
| lęgan, *lay* | ę (Mut.) < æ < a | Go. lagjan |
| sęndan, *send* | ę (Mut.) < ǫ (Infl.-N) < a | Go. sandjan |
| męrgen, *morrow* | ę (Mut.) < o | Go. maúrgins |
| | | (§ 113) |
| | | |
| **i** | | |
| hit, *it* | i < i | Go. ita |
| miht, *canst* | i (Mut. Pal.) < ea (Brkᵍ) < æ < a | OHG. maht |
| niman, *take* | i (Infl.-N) < e | OHG. neman |
| six, *six* | i (Mut. Pal.) < eo (Brkᵍ) < e | OHG. sehs |
| betwih, *between* | i (Shortᵍ) < ī | cp. Go. tweihnái |
| | | (§ 113) |

[1] OHG. = Old High German, OS. = Old Saxon, I. = Icelandic, Go. = Gothic, Germ. = Germanic.

## o

| | | |
|---|---|---|
| gold, *gold* | o < o | OHG. gold |
| sworen, *sworn* | o (W-Infl.) < a | Go. swarans – |
| LWS. worc, *work* | o (W-Infl.) < eo (Brk⁵) < e | OHG. werk |
| swostor, *sister* | o (W-Infl.) < eo (U-Mut.) < e | OHG. swester – |
| orlege, *war* | o < u | OS. urlogi |

## ǫ

| | | |
|---|---|---|
| hǫnd, *hand* | ǫ (Infl.-N) < a | Go. handus |

## u

| | | |
|---|---|---|
| sunu, *son* | u < u | Go. sunus |
| LWS. swustor, *sister* | u (W-Infl.) < eo (U-Mut.) < e | OHG. swester |
| LWS. swurd, *sword* | u (W-Infl.) < eo (Brk⁵) < e | OHG. swert |
| wudu, *wood* | u (W-Infl.) < io (U-Mut.) < i | OHG. witu |
| wulf, *wolf* | u < o | OHG. wolf – ? |
| cumen (pp.), *come* | u (Infl.-N) < o | OHG. quoman |
| bet(w)uh, *between* | u (W-Infl.) < io (Brk⁵) < i (Short⁵) < ī | cp. Go. tweihnái |

## y

| | | |
|---|---|---|
| cyssan, *kiss* | y (Mut.) < u | OS. kussian |

## ea

| | | |
|---|---|---|
| cearu, *care* | ea (U-Mut.) < a | OHG. chara |
| feax, *hair* | ea (Brk⁵) < æ < a | OHG. fahs |
| geaf, *gave* | ea (Pal. Diph.) < æ < a | Go. gaf |
| sceacan, *shake* | ea (Pal. Diph.) < a | I. skaka |

## eo

| | | |
|---|---|---|
| sweostor, *sister* | eo (U-Mut.) < e | OHG. swester |
| weorc, *work* | eo (Brk⁵) < e | OHG. werk |
| sceomu, *shame* | eo (Pal. Diph.) < ǫ (Infl.-N) < a | OHG. scama |
| sceop, *bard* | eo (Pal. Diph.) < o | OHG. scof |
| sceolon, *shall* | eo (Pal. Diph.) < u | Go. skulun |
| leoht, *not heavy* | eo (Brk⁵) < i (Short⁵) < ī | Go. leihts |

## ie

| | | |
|---|---|---|
| bieldu, *boldness* | ie (Mut.) < ea (Brk⁶)  <br>         < æ < a | Go. balþei |
| giest, *guest* | ie (Mut.) < ea (Pal. Diph.)  <br>         < æ < a | Go. gasti-[1] |
| siex, *six* | ie (Mut. Pal.) < eo (Brk⁶)  <br>         < e | OHG. sehs |
| giefan, *give* | ie (Pal. Diph.) < e | OHG. geban |
| hierde, *(shep)herd* | ie (Mut.) < io (Brk⁶) < i | OHG. hirti |
| bierð, *bears* | ie (Glide-Diph.) < i | OS. birid |

## io

| | | |
|---|---|---|
| siolofr, *silver* | io (U-Mut.) < i | Go. silubr |
| miox, *ordure* | io (Brk⁶) < i | OHG. mist |
| gioc, geoc, *yoke* | io (Pal. Diph.) < o | OHG. johh |
| giong, geong, *young* | io (Pal. Diph.) < u | Go. juggs |

## Long Vowels.

### ā

| | | |
|---|---|---|
| hāl, *whole* | ā < ai | Go. hails |
| sāwon, *saw* | ā < W. Germ. ā < Germ. æ | Go. sēhwun |
| hwā, *who* | ā (Length⁶) < a | Go. hwas |

### ǣ

| | | |
|---|---|---|
| lǣtan, *let* | ǣ < W. Germ. ā < Germ. æ | Go. lētan (§ 113) |
| lǣwan, *betray* | ǣ (Mut.) < W. Germ. ā <  <br>    Germ. æ | Go. lēwjan |
| rǣran, *rear* | ǣ (Mut.) < ā < ai | Go. ráisjan |
| sǣde, *said* | ǣ (Loss-G) < æ < a | OHG. sagēta |

---

[1] Forms ending with hyphens are stems. The stem gives the clue to the *I*-Mutation; the nom. sg. does not.

## ē

| | | |
|---|---|---|
| hēr, *here* | ē < ē̄ | Go. hēr |
| fēhð, *seizes* | ē (Mut.) < ō (Infl.-*N*) < ā | Go. fāhiþ |
| cwēn, *woman* | ē (Mut.) < ō (Infl.-*N*) < W. Germ. ā < Germ. æ | Go. qēns (§ 113) |
| gēr, *year* | ē (Pal. Mon.) < ēa (Pal. Diph.) < ǣ < W. Germ. ā < Germ. ǣ | Go. jēr (§ 113) |
| sēcan, *seek* | ē (Mut.) < ō | OS. sōkian |
| LWS. tēh, *drew* | ē (Mut. Pal.) < ēa < au | Go. táuh |
| LWS. gēt, *poured* | ē (Pal. Mon.) < ēa < au | Go. gáut |
| genēðan, *venture* | ē (Mut.) < ō (Loss-*N*) < ǫ (Infl.-*N*) < a | Go. gananþjan |
| lēde, *laid* | ē (Loss-*G*) < ę (Mut.) < æ < a | Go. lagida |
| ongēn, *against* | ē (Pal. Mon.) < ēa (Loss-*G*) < ea (Pal. Diph.) < æ < a | OHG. ingagan |
| ðēn, *thane* | ē (Loss-*G*) < e | OS. thegan |
| wē, *we* | ē (Length$^g$) < e < i | OHG. wir |

## ī

| | | |
|---|---|---|
| wīs, *wise* | ī < ī̄ | OHG. wīsi |
| fīf, *five* | ī (Loss-*N*) < i | Go. fimf |
| brīdels, *bridle* | ī (Loss-*G*) < i | OHG. brittel |
| bī, *by* | ī (Length$^g$) < i | Go. bi |

## ō

| | | |
|---|---|---|
| gōd, *good* | ō < ō̄ | Go. gōds |
| fōn, *seize* | ō (Infl.-*N*) < ā | Go., OHG. fāhan |
| cōmon, *came* | ō (Infl.-*N*) < W. Germ. ā < Germ. ǣ | Go. qēmun (§ 113) |
| gōs, *goose* | ō (Loss-*N*) < ǫ (Infl.-*N*) < a | OHG. gans |
| brōden, *braided* | ō (Loss-*G*) < o | OHG. gibrottan |
| hōles, *of a hole* | ō (Loss-*H*) < o | cp. OHG. hol |

### ū

| | | |
|---|---|---|
| lūcan, *lock* | ū < ū | Go. galūkan |
| hūsl, *eucharist* | ū (Loss-N) < u | Go. hunsl |
| brūdon, *shook* | ū (Loss-G) < u | OHG. brutton |
| ðū, *thou* | ū (Length⁵) < u | Go. þu |

### ȳ

| | | |
|---|---|---|
| brȳd, *bride* | ȳ (Mut.) < ū | Go. brūdi- |
| cȳdan, *make known* | ȳ (Mut.) < ū (Loss-N) < u | Go. kunþjan |
| oferhȳd, *arrogance* | ȳ (Loss-G) < y (Mut.) < u | cp. Go. hugs |
| ðȳrel, *hole* | ȳ (Loss-H) < y (Mut.) < u | cp. OHG. thuruh |

### ēa

| | | |
|---|---|---|
| tēah, *drew* | ēa < au | Go. táuh |
| gēar, *year* | ēa (Pal. Diph.) < ǣ < W. Germ. ā < Germ. ǣ | Go. jēr (§ 113) |
| nēar, *nearer* | ēa (Contr.) < W. Germ. ā < Germ. ǣ | Go. nēhwōz (§ 113) |
| scēadan, *separate* | ēa (Pal. Diph.) < ā < ai | Go. skáidan |
| fēawe, *few* | ēa < au (Infl.-W) < a | Go. fawai |
| ēa, *water* | ēa (Contr.) < a | Go. ahwa |
| Wēalas, *Britons* | ēa (Loss-H) < ea (Brk⁵) < æ < a | OHG. walh (sing.) |
| ongēan, *against* | ēa (Loss-G) < ea (Pal. Diph.) < æ < a | OHG. ingagan |

10—2

## ēo

| | | |
|---|---|---|
| cēosan, *choose* | ēo < eu | Go. kiusan (§ 113) |
| gēomor, *sad* | ēo (Pal. Diph.) < ō (Infl.-*N*) < W. Germ. ā < Germ. ǣ | OS. jāmar |
| scēop, *created* | ēo (Pal. Diph.) < ō | Go. gaskōp |
| scēofan, *shove* | ēo (Pal. Diph.) < ū | I. skūfa |
| mēowle, *girl* | ēo (Infl.-*W*) < ę (Mut.) < æ < a | Go. mawilō |
| fēolan, *penetrate* | ēo (Loss-*H*) < eo (Brk$^g$) < e | Go. filhan (§ 113) |
| cnēowes, *of a knee* | ēo < eu (Infl.-*W*) < e | OHG. knewes |
| sēon, *see* | ēo (Contr.) < e | Go. saíhwan |
| gēo, *formerly* | ēo (Pal. Diph.) < ū (Length$^g$) < u | Go. ju |

## īe

| | | |
|---|---|---|
| cīest, *chooses* | īe (Mut.) < iu | Go. kiusiþ |
| hīeran, *hear* | īe (Mut.) < ēa < au | Go. hausjan |
| cīese, *cheese* | īe (Mut.) < ēa (Pal. Diph.) < ǣ < W. Germ. ā | OHG. kāsi |
| wīelisc, *foreign* | īe (Loss-*H*) < ie (Mut.) < ea (Brk$^g$) < æ < a | OHG. walhisc |
| sīe, *be* | īe (Contr.) < i | Go. sijái |
| frīend, *friends* | īe (Mut.) < īo (Contr.) < i | Go. frijōnds |

## īo

| | | |
|---|---|---|
| ðīon (ðēon), *thrive* | īo (Contr.) < ī | OS. thīhan |
| frīond (frēond), *friend* | īo (Contr.) < i | Go. frijōnds |

# CONSONANTS.

**164.** Anything like a full treatment of the history of the OE. consonants is beyond the scope of this book. Some changes that they undergo have been referred to in the preceding pages: in some cases, nothing need be added to what is there said; in a few others, it will be a gain to collect similar phenomena. This is done under the headings: I. Loss; II. Assimilation; III. Metathesis; IV. Doubling; V. Verner's Law.

## I. LOSS.

**165.** (i) The simplification of double consonants is the rule at the end of a word. In inflected forms it is sufficiently dealt with in the Accidence.

(ii) Loss of medial $g$, $h$, $j$, $m$, $n$, and $w$, leading to Contraction and Compensatory Lengthening, is fully treated in the sections on the Sound-Laws.

(iii) $W$ is usually lost when final.

(*a*) After a short vowel it is vocalised to $u$, and the two vowels form a diphthong: *\*trew* > *\*treu* > *trēo*, tree; but it is apt to be restored from the oblique cases: *trēow*.

(*b*) After a long vowel it remains in some words, disappears in others: *sǣ*, sea; *hrā*, corpse; *snāw*, snow; but here again it is often restored from the inflected forms: *hrāw*.

(*c*) After consonants $w > u$: *bearu*, grove; which was lost, according to the usual rule (§ 9), after a long syllable: *mǣd*, meadow.

Besides the loss in Contraction, medial $w$ disappears in a number of words, of which the following will serve as examples: negative forms of *wesan* (be), *witan* (know), *willan* (will): *næs*, etc.; *tū*, neut. of *twēgen*, two; *betux* ∝ *betwux*, between; *gierede*, past of *gierwan*, prepare.

## II. ASSIMILATION.

**166.** The following cases are worthy of note:

(*a*) *d* > *t* before and after a voiceless consonant: in the 2nd and 3rd sing. indic. of verbs, and in the past tenses of weak verbs of Class I. (§§ 69, 88); and in *blētsian*, bless (cp. *blōd*), etc.

(*b*) ð > *t* in the 2nd (*rīdest* < *rīdesð* < *rīdes ðū*) and 3rd sing. pres. indic. (§ 69); in *ðætte* (< *ðæt ðe*), that (conj.); *ēaðmēttu*, humility; *gīemeliest*, neglect, etc.

(*c*) ðs > ss in *bliss*, joy, *liss*, grace; cp. *blīðe*, joyous, *līðe*, gentle.

(*d*) sr > ss in *læssa*, compar. of *lȳtel*, little; *ðisse*, *ðissa*, in the declension of *ðes*, this.

## III. METATHESIS.

**167.** The only metathesis that need be mentioned here is that of *r*, which is somewhat frequent, especially before *nn* and covered *s*: *burna* (< *\*brunna*), spring; *bærnan* (< *\*brannjan*), burn (trans.); *bi(e)rnan* (< *\*brinnan*), burn (intrans.); *i(e)rnan* (< *rinnan*), run; *berstan* (< *\*brestan*), burst; *ðerscan* (< *\*ðrescan*), thresh; *hors* (< *\*hross*), horse; *gærs* (< *\*gras*), grass, etc.

## IV. GEMINATION.

**168.** The W. Germanic gemination before *j* has been referred to in the Accidence. After a short vowel every consonant, except *r*, was doubled before *j*; subsequently this *j* mutated the root vowel, and then dropped. Hence such forms as those of the "weak presents" (§ 80) of Classes V. and VI., and many other words:

| | | |
|---|---|---|
| hębban, *raise* | hliehhan, *laugh* | scieppan, *create* |
| ręccan, *relate* | tęllan, *tell* | cnyssan, *thrust* |
| hręddan, *rescue* | fręmman, *perform* | sęttan, *set* |
| bycgan, *buy* | dyn(n), *din* | sceððan, *injure* |
| hrycg, *back* | węnnan, *accustom* | |

## V. VERNER'S LAW.

**169.** An interchange of consonants is seen in the parts of all contracted strong verbs and of some other strong verbs, the explanation of which must be sought in the Germanic period. Primitive Germanic *f*, *h*, þ[1], *s* (< Indo-Germ. *p*, *k*, *t*, *s*), remained unchanged only when the vowel next preceding bore the principal accent; otherwise, i.e. if the vowel next preceding did not bear the principal accent of the word, *f*, *h*, þ[1], *s* > *r*, *g*, ð[1], *z*. In Late Germanic, as in OE., the principal accent fell on the root-syllable; but in the Primitive Germanic period the accent might fall on any syllable. This fact is illustrated in the strong verbs, in which the present forms and the past sing. indic. had the principal accent on the root-syllable, whereas all the other past forms had the principal accent on the ending. Therefore the present and the past sing. of strong verbs retained the voiceless spirants *s*, þ[1], *h*, *f* (= OE. *s*, ð, *h*, *f*), which in all the other past forms became *z*, ð[1], *g*, *v* (= OE. *r*, *d*, *g*, *f*). This law was discovered and formulated by Karl Verner of Copenhagen in 1875, and has never been questioned since. Its operation is often referred to by the ambiguous term "grammatical change."

OE. has not separate symbols for the sounds of *f* and *v*, and therefore the changes that are explained by Verner's Law can only be seen in the interchange of the following pairs of consonants:

(*a*) s : r
(*b*) ð : d
(*c*) h : g
(*d*) h(w) : (g)w *or* g(w)

The verbs that come under this law and those in which the law fails have been indicated in the Accidence; therefore only a few examples are needed here.

[1] Here þ and ð are used with their proper phonetic value, þ voiceless (= th) and ð voiced (= dh).

(a)  s : r

Class II ("Creep"): cēosan, *choose*    cēas̱    cuṟon    coren
„   V ("Tread"): wesan, *be*    wæs    wǣron

In *genesan*, to survive, the law fails, but is seen in the derivative verb *generian*, to save.

(b)  ð : d

Class I ("Shine"): sníðan, *cut*    snáð    snidon    sniden
   Cp. snide, *cutting*.
Class V ("Tread"): cweðan, *say*    cwæð    cwǣdon    cweden
   Cp. cwide, *speech*.

(c)  h : g

All strong contracted verbs (§ 81) belong here, except *sēon*, see; but those of Classes VI. and VII. were apt to borrow the *g* of the past pl. in the past sing.

Class VI ("Fare"): slēan, *strike*    slōg    slōgon    slægen

   Cp. *slege*, stroke, and *slaga*, slayer. And the "weak present" of the same class:

         hliehhan, *laugh*    hlōg    hlōgon

(d)  h(w) : (g)w *or* g(w)

Class V ("Tread"): sēon, *see*    seah    { sāwon    sewen
                                    { sǣgon    segen

NOTE. Final *g* often > *h* after *ā*, *ō*, and sometimes after *l* or *r*, but this has nothing to do with Verner's Law. Thus *slōg* > *slōh*; *stāg* > *stāh* (ascended); *burg* > *burh* (stronghold).

# APPENDIX.

## I. FORMATION OF ADVERBS.

**170.** Adverbs formed from Adjectives usually end in -e and are identical with the instrumental sing. of the adj.:

| adj. | adv. | adj. | adv. |
|---|---|---|---|
| dēop | dēope, *deeply* | blīðe | blīðe, *blithely* |
| long | longe, *long, far* | clǣne | clǣne, *clean* |
| swīð | swīðe, *strongly, very* | dēoplīc | dēoplīce, *deeply* |
| wīd | wīde, *widely* | glædlīc | glædlīce, *gladly* |
| nearu | nearwe, *narrowly* | heardlīc | heardlīce, *severely* |
| hlūtor | hlūtre, *brightly* | sōðlīc | sōðlīce, *truly* |

NOTES. (1) In the last four examples, the simple adjs., *dēop, glæd, heard, sōð*, are also found. Hence -*līce* came to be regarded as an adverbial termination, was added to adjs. that had not forms in -*līc*, and finally, in the Middle English period, supplemented the less distinct adverbial ending -*e*. Exs.:

| | |
|---|---|
| blīðe | blīðelīce, *joyously* |
| rōt | rōtlīce, *gladly* |
| sweotol | sweotollīce, *clearly* |

(2) Three adjs., which are *i*- or *j*-stems, have therefore mutated vowels, whereas the advs. keep the original vowel:

| | |
|---|---|
| sēfte | sōfte, *softly* |
| smēðe | smōðe, *smoothly* |
| swēte | swōte, *sweetly* |

**171.** The oblique cases of adjs. and nouns are used adverbially.

(1) **Accusative** (neut. of adj.):

eall, *entirely*  
full, *fully*  
genōg, *enough*  
lyt(el), *little*  
hwōn, *somewhat*  
ealne weg, *always*  
ðā hwīle (ðe), *while*  
norð, *north*  
norðweard, *northwards*  
ūpweard, *upwards*  

(2) **Genitive**:

ealles, *altogether*  
nealles, *not at all*  
hāmweardes, *homewards*  
norðweardes, *northwards*  
dæges, *by day*  
nihtes, *by night*  
niedes, *needs*  
ðonces, *willingly*  
ungewealdes, *involuntarily*  

and even compounded with a preposition:

tō-middes, *in the midst*

(3) **Dative** (Instr.), sing. and pl.:

elne, *courageously*  
fācne, *excessively*  
hwēne, *somewhat*  
miclum, *very*  
hwīlum, *sometimes*  
hwīltīdum, *sometimes*  
wundrum, *wondrous(ly)*  
floccmǣlum, *in troops*  
styccemǣlum, *piecemeal, here and there*


**172.** Other adverbial terminations are -*a* and -*unga* (-*inga*):

gēara, *of yore*  
sōna, *soon*  
tela, *well*  
tuwa, *twice*  
ðriwa, *thrice*  
ānunga, *once for all*  
eallunga, *altogether*  
ierringa, *angrily*  
grundlunga, *from the foundations*

**173.** The chief adverbs of place are:

| Rest | Motion towards | Motion from |
|---|---|---|
| hēr, *here* | hider | heonan |
| hwǣr, *where?* | hwider | hwonan |
| ðær, *there* | ðider | ðonan |
| inne, innan, *within* | in(n) | innan |
| ūte, ūtan, *outside* | ūt | ūtan |
| uppe, uppan, *up, above* | ūp | |
| ufan, *above* | | ufan |
| neoðan, *beneath* | niðer | neoðan |
| foran, fore, *before* | forð | |
| hindan, *behind* | hinder | hindan |
| feorr(an), *far, afar* | feor(r) | feorran |
| nēah, *near* | | nēan |
| | norð, *north* | norðan |
| | sūð, *south* | sūðan |
| | eāst, *east* | ēastan |
| | west, *west* | westan |

## II. PREFIXES.

**174.** The following are the principal OE. prefixes, with selected examples.

**ā-**: (1) unstressed form of *or-*, away, and then merely intensive: *āfaran*, to depart; *ārīsan*, to arise; *ābēodan*, to order.

(2) weakened from *on-*: *āweg*, away.

(3) shortened from *āwa*, ever, 'any-': *āhwǣr*, anywhere, everywhere (§ 62).

**ǣ-**, a privative prefix, 'without': *ǣmōd*, discouraged; *ǣswind*, idle.

**æf**, rare stressed form of *of-*, 'off, from': *æfweard*, absent; *æfðonc*, grudge.

**æfter-**, 'after': *æfterboren*, posthumous; *æfterfylgend*, follower.

**ǣg-** (< *ǣgi-*), 'every-': *ǣghwǣr*, everywhere (§ 62).

**æt-**, 'at, from': *ætwītan*, to twit; *ætsomne*, together; *ætniman*, to take away.

**be-**, unstressed form of *bī-*, 'by, about':

(*a*) specialises the meanings of transitive verbs: *besęttan*, to beset; *besēcan*, to beseech.

(*b*) makes intrans. verbs transitive: *bescīnan*, to illuminate; *berīdan*, to encompass.

(*c*) privative: *bedǣlan*, *belīsan*, *benǣman*, *beniman*, *bescierian*, *besnyðian*, to deprive of.

(*d*) without assignable force: *bebēodan*, to command; *bescūfan*, to shove.

**bī-**, 'by' (see *be-*): *bīleofa*, sustenance; *bīspell*, example.

**ed-**, 're-': *edlēan*, reward; *ednīwian*, to renew.

**for-**: (1) earlier unstressed form *fer-*, distinct from prep. *for*; denotes loss, destruction; intensifies; deteriorates; negatives:

| | |
|---|---|
| fordōn, *to destroy* | forgiefan, *to forgive* |
| forweorðan, *to perish* | forbærnan, *to burn up* |
| forwyrd, *destruction* | fretan (<*for-etan), *to devour* |
| forspillan, *to destroy* | forsēon, *to despise* |
| forgān, *to forgo* | forswerian, *to swear falsely* |
| forgietan, *to forget* | forbēodan, *to forbid* |

(2) = the prep. *for*: *forstǫndan*, to defend; *forfaran*, *forrīdan*, to intercept.

**fore-**, 'fore-': *forecweðan*, to foretell; *foreðǫnc*, forethought; *foremǣre*, very great.

**ge-**: (*a*) originally = together (L. cum), as in *gefēre*, company; *gefēgan*, to fit together (§ 62).

(*b*) makes intrans. verbs transitive, often with the added notion of attainment, gain, success: *gewinnan*, to win, cp. *winnan*, to fight; *geærnan*, to gain by galloping, cp. *ærnan*, to gallop; *geāscian*, to learn by asking, hear of.

(*c*) initial inflection of past participles: *gebiden*, *gelōcod*.

(*d*) very often without assignable meaning: *gebēodan*, to order; *gebedhūs*, chapel.

**in-**, 'in': *ingǫng*, ingress; *infyrdian*, to invade.

**mid-**[1], 'with': *midwyrhta*, cooperator.

---

[1] *Mid-* frequently = 'mid-,' as in *midniht*, but can then hardly be regarded as a mere prefix.

§ 174 PREFIXES. 157

**mis-**, 'mis-': *mislimpan*, to go wrong; *misdǣd*, misdeed.

**n-**, negative prefix: *nis*, is not; *nān*, none.

**of-**, unstressed form of *æf-*, which it almost entirely displaced:

(*a*) originally = off: *ofspring*, offspring; *ofāslēan*, to smite off; *oftēon*, to withhold.

(*b*) intensive: *ofstingan*, to stab to death; *oftorfian*, to stone to death.

(*c*) makes intrans. verbs trans., often specialising the meaning:

  ofsittan, *to oppress*     offeallan, *to fall upon*
  offaran, *to overtake*     ofðyncan, *to displease*.

**ofer-**: (*a*) = over: *oferstīgan*, to surmount; *oferswīðan*, to overpower; *ofersprǣce*, loquacious.

(*b*) with negative force: *ofergietan*, to forget; *ofersittan*, to abstain from.

**on** (an)-: (1) unstressed form of *ǫnd-*, denotes reversal, change:

  onlūcan, *to unlock*     onwindan, *to unwind*
  onhlīdan, ontynan, *to open*   onwęndan, *to change, upset*

(2) = the prep. 'on':

  onwinnan, *to assail*     onlīchtan, *to illuminate*
  onsittan, *to occupy*     onslǣpan, *to fall asleep*
  onǣlan, *to ignite*      ongēan, *against*.

(3) often without assignable meaning: *onginnan*, to begin.

**ǫnd** (and)-, stressed form of *on* (Greek ἀντί), back: *ǫndwyrde*, answer.

**or-**, stressed form of *ā-* (1); see § 104 N.

**oð-**, 'away'; *oðfeallan*, to fall off; *oðhealdan*, to keep back.

**sǫm** (sam)-, 'together': *sǫmwist*, a living together.

**sōm** (sām)-, 'half': *sōmwīs*, stupid; *sōmworht*, half-made.

**tō-**: (1) = earlier *te-*, L. dis-, 'asunder'; *tōbregdan*, *toslītan*, to tear to pieces; *tōfaran*, *tōfēran*, to disperse.

(2) = *tō* (prep.): *tōgēanes*, towards; *tōcyme*, arrival; *tōweard*, future.

**ðurh-**, 'through': *ðurhtēon*, to accomplish.

**un-**: (*a*) = 'un-': *unrōt*, sad; *uncūð*, unknown; *ungewisses*, unconsciously.

(*b*) pejorative: *untydre*, evil progeny.

**under-**, 'under': *understọndan*, to understand.

**wan-**, 'un-': *wanhāl*, unhealthy; *wansǣlig*, unhappy.

**wið-**, 'with-, against': *wiðstọndan*, to withstand; *wiðfeohtend*, adversary.

**wiðer-**, 'against, re-': *wiðerflita*, *wiðerwinna*, opponent, adversary; *wiðerstal*, resistance.

**ymb** (ymbe)-, 'around': *ymbsittan*, invest; *ymbeðọnc*, reflection.

## III. SUFFIXES.

**175.** The principal OE. suffixes (except adverbial, see §§ 170—3) are here given in one list in alphabetical order. Some of the suffixes included existed also as independent words in OE., and might more correctly be regarded as forming compounds; but compounds pass into derivatives in the course of time, and it has been thought better to err, if at all, on the side of inclusion.

**-að** (oð), noun masc., abstract: *fiscað*, fishing; *huntoð*, hunting.

**-bǣre**, adj., 'bearing': *wæstmbǣre*, fruitful; *lustbǣre*, desirable.

**-cund**, adj. denoting nature: *godcund*, divine; *heofoncund*, heavenly.

**-dōm**, '-dom,' noun masc., usu. abstract: *frēodōm*, freedom; *lǣcedōm*, medicine.

**-els**, noun masc.: *byrgels*, tomb; *rēcels*, incense.

**-en** (1), noun neut., sometimes dimin.: *cliewen*, sphere; *cycen*, chicken.

**-en** (2), noun fem., often a person: *gyden*, goddess; *byrgen*, tomb.

**-en** (3), adj. of material etc.: *gylden*, golden: *hǣðen*, heathen.

**-(e)nd**, noun masc., agent: *āgend*, owner; *Scieppend*, Creator; *frēond*, friend.

**-ere**, '-er,' noun masc., agent: *bōcere*, scribe; *fiscere*, fisher; *godspellere*, evangelist.

**-ern**, noun neut., 'house': *horsern*, stable; *blācern*, lantern.

**-erne**, '-ern,' adj., local: *norðerne*, northern.

**-estre**, '-ster,' noun fem., person: *webbestre*, spinster; *witegestre*, prophetess.

**-ettan**, verb: *licettan*, to feign.

**-fæst**, '-fast,' adj.: *stedefæst*, steadfast; *scomfæst*, shamefast.

**-feald**, '-fold,' adj.: *monigfeald*, manifold; *ðritigfeald*, thirtyfold.

**-full**, '-ful,' adj.: *cearfull*, anxious; *synnfull*, guilty.

**-hād**, '-hood,' noun masc., abstract: *cildhād*, childhood: *mægdenhād*, virginity.

**-ig**, '-y,' adj.: *hālig*, holy; *mōdig*, proud; *welig*, wealthy.

**-iht**, adj.: *heoruhōciht*, savagely barbed; *hrēodiht*, reedy.

**-ing**, noun masc.; (*a*) patronymic: *æðeling*, prince; *Æðelwulfing*, son of Ethelwulf.

(*b*) without assignable force: *ierming*, poor wretch; *hæring*, herring; *scilling*, shilling.

**-isc**, '-ish,' adj.: *Englisc*, English; *wielisc*, foreign; *cildisc*, childish.

**-lāc**, '-lock,' noun neut., abstract: *feohtlāc*, fighting; *wedlāc*, wedlock.

**-lǣcan**, verb: *nēalǣcan*, to approach; *ðristlǣcan*, to embolden.

**-lēas**, '-less,' adj.: *giemelēas*, heedless; *rēcelēas*, reckless.

**-līc**, '-ly,' adj.: *gōdlīc*, goodly; *wīflīc*, womanly; *unāberendlīc*, intolerable; *ungesewenlīc*, invisible.

**-liest** (lēast), '-lessness,' noun fem., abstract: *giemeliest*, negligence; *slǣpliest*, sleeplessness.

**-ling**, '-ling,' noun masc., dimin., or denoting affection or contempt: *dēorling*, darling; *geongling*, youth; *hȳrling*, hireling.

N.B. On *bæcling*, on *hinderling*, backwards.

**-mōd**, '-minded,' adj.: *ēaðmōd*, humble-minded.

**-nes**, '-ness,' noun fem., abstract: *gōdnes*, goodness; *forsewennes*, contempt.

**-ol**, adj.: *sticol*, rough; *swicol*, deceitful.

**-rǣden**, noun fem., abstract: *mǣgrǣden*, relationship; *gecwedrǣden*, agreement; *monrǣden*, homage.

**-rīce**, '-ric,' noun neut.: *biscoprīce*, bishopric; *cynerīce*, kingdom.

-scipe, '-ship,' noun masc., abstract: *frēondscipe*, friendship; *hwætscipe*, boldness.

-sian, verb: *blētsian*, to bless; *clǣnsian*, to cleanse.

-stafas, noun masc. pl., abstract: *ārstafas*, favour; *fācenstafas*, treachery.

-sum, '-some,' adj.: *wynsum*, winsome; *lǫngsum*, tedious.

-tīeme, adj.: *hefigtīeme*, grievous; *ðwēortīeme*, perverse.

-ð(u), '-th,' noun fem., abstract: *strengð(u)*, strength; *fǣhð*, hostility.

-u (preceded by mutated root-vowel), noun fem., abstract: *hǣlu*, health; *menigu*, multitude.

-ung (ing), '-ing,' noun fem., abstract: *blētsung*, blessing; *miltsung*, mercy.

-weard, '-ward,' adj., local and temporal: *norðweard*, northward: *tōweard*, future.

-wende, adj.: *hālwende*, healthy; *hwīlwende*, transitory.

-weorð, wierðe, '-worthy,' adj.: *ārweorð*, venerable; *tǣlwierðe*, blameworthy; *untǣlwierðe*, blameless.

-wīs, adj.: *rihtwīs*, righteous; *ungescēadwīs*, unintelligent.

---

CAMBRIDGE: PRINTED BY J. AND C. F. CLAY, AT THE UNIVERSITY PRESS.

www.ingramcontent.com/pod-product-compliance
Lightning Source LLC
Chambersburg PA
CBHW020305170426
43202CB00008B/502